FIRST-TIMER? NEWBIE?

NOT TO WORRY. ...

The manga you are about to read v... you may know, Japanese reads right-to-... ould go through this whole elaborate proc... nse to force a left-to-right reading, but isn... it much cooler to experience it as close to the original as possible?

Things might be a bit disconcerting at first, but you're sharp. You'll catch on quick. If you find you're getting lost, refer to the handy diagram.

Got it? Good! Now read to your heart's content, and when you're finished, find a friend who's never read manga before and show them how it's done!

RATING SUMMARY

The goal of the Yen Press rating system is provide parents, librarians and retailers with as much information about the contents of our books as simply and concisely as possible. Ultimately, opinions about appropriateness of content for a particular reader are a subjective matter likely to vary from person to person. However, this is a useful tool to give readers some sense of what they may expect.

Yen's ratings are structured in two tiers: age ratings (A, T, OT, M) and content indicators (L, V, S, N). Age ratings indicate a maturity threshold below which some parents or guardians may find the content unsuitable. Content indicators provide insight as to the material within the book that prompted a particular age rating. The frequency and/or severity of that material is reflected in the age rating.

AGE RATINGS

 A = All Ages
An "A" rating indicates that the material contained within the book has been deemed unlikely to be found inappropriate for any particular age group.

 T = Teen
A "T" rating indicates that there may be content within a book that some parents or guardians may consider inappropriate for children under the age of 13.

 OT = Older Teen
An "OT" rated book contains material that some parents or guardians may consider inappropriate for readers under the age of 16.

 M = Mature
An "M" rated book is intended for a mature readership and may be considered inappropriate for readers under the age of 18.

CONTENT INDICATORS

L = Language
V = Violence
S = Sexual Situations
N = Nudity

FROM SVETLANA CHMAKOVA
Bestselling creator of DRAMACON

"Because vampires need calculus, too."

Nightschool

COMING 2008   FROM YEN PRESS

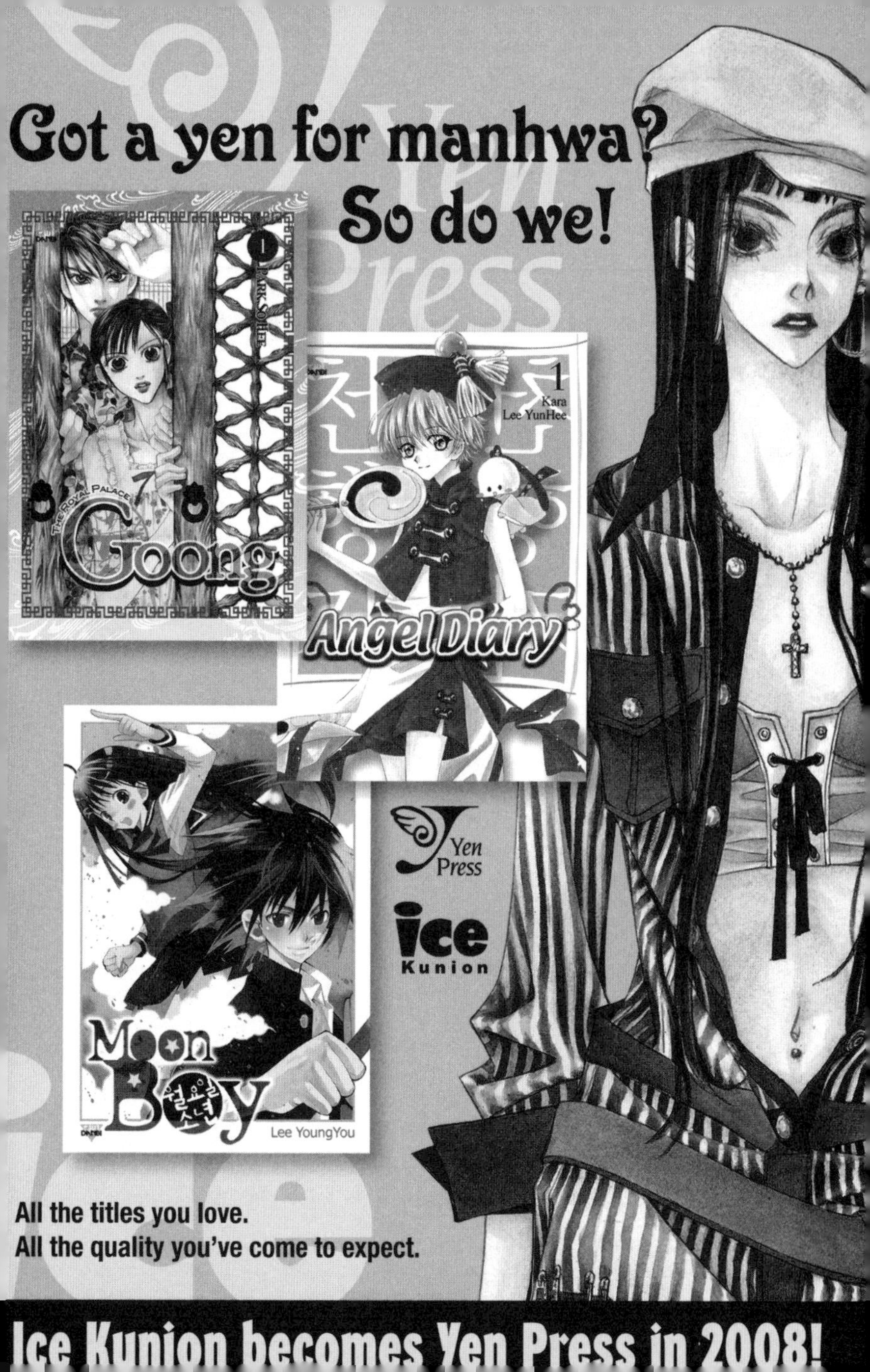
Got a yen for manhwa?
So do we!
1
PARK SoHee
THE ROYAL PALACE
Goong
1
Kara
Lee YunHee
Angel Diary
Yen Press
ice
Kunion
Moon Boy
월요일 소년
Lee YoungYou
All the titles you love.
All the quality you've come to expect.
Ice Kunion becomes Yen Press in 2008!

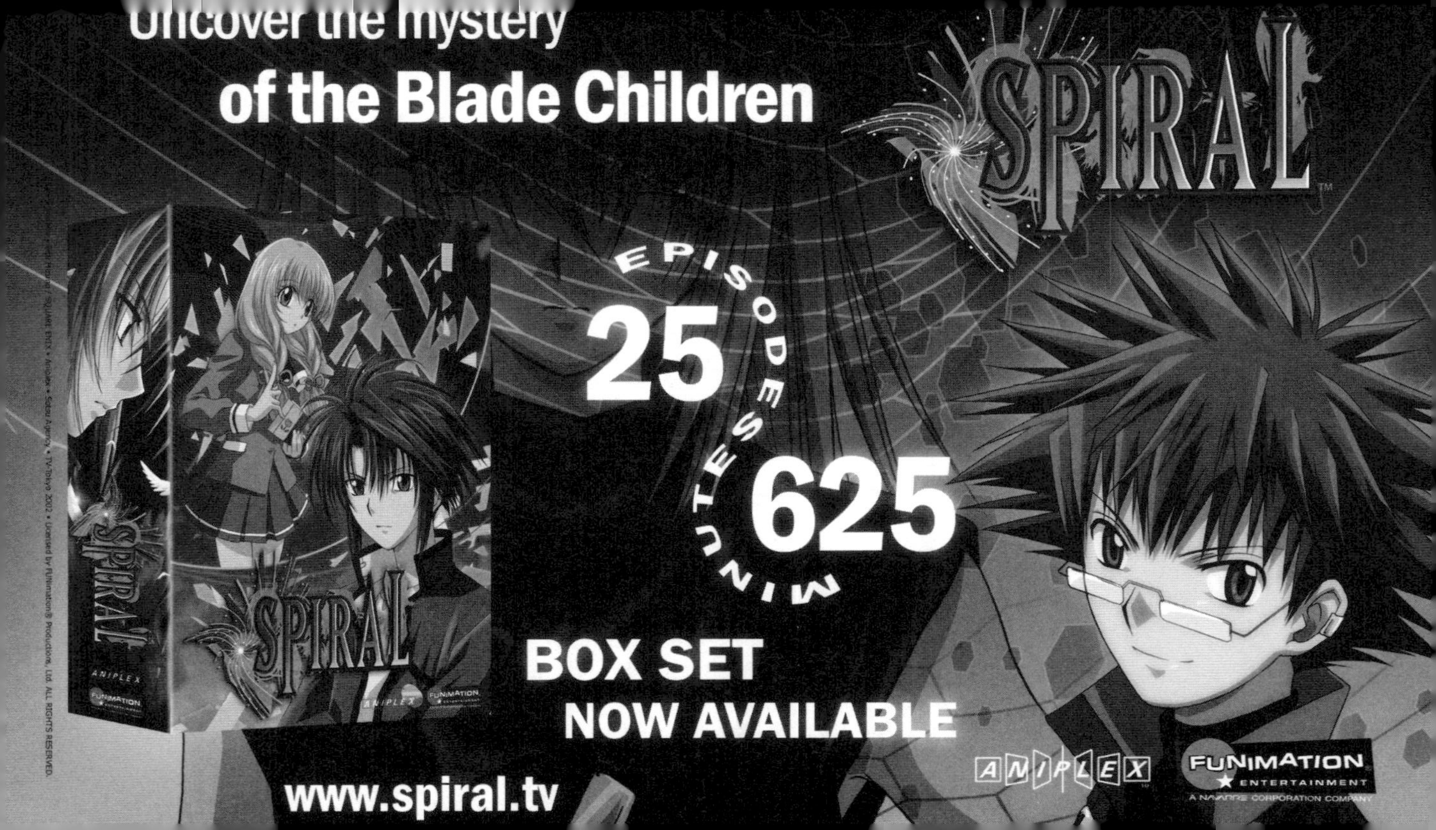
Uncover the mystery
of the Blade Children
SPIRAL™
25 EPISODES
625 MINUTES
BOX SET
NOW AVAILABLE
www.spiral.tv
ANIPLEX
FUNIMATION ENTERTAINMENT
A NAVARRE CORPORATION COMPANY
Sotsu Agency • TV-Tokyo 2002 • Licensed by FUNimation® Productions, Ltd. ALL RIGHTS RESERVED.

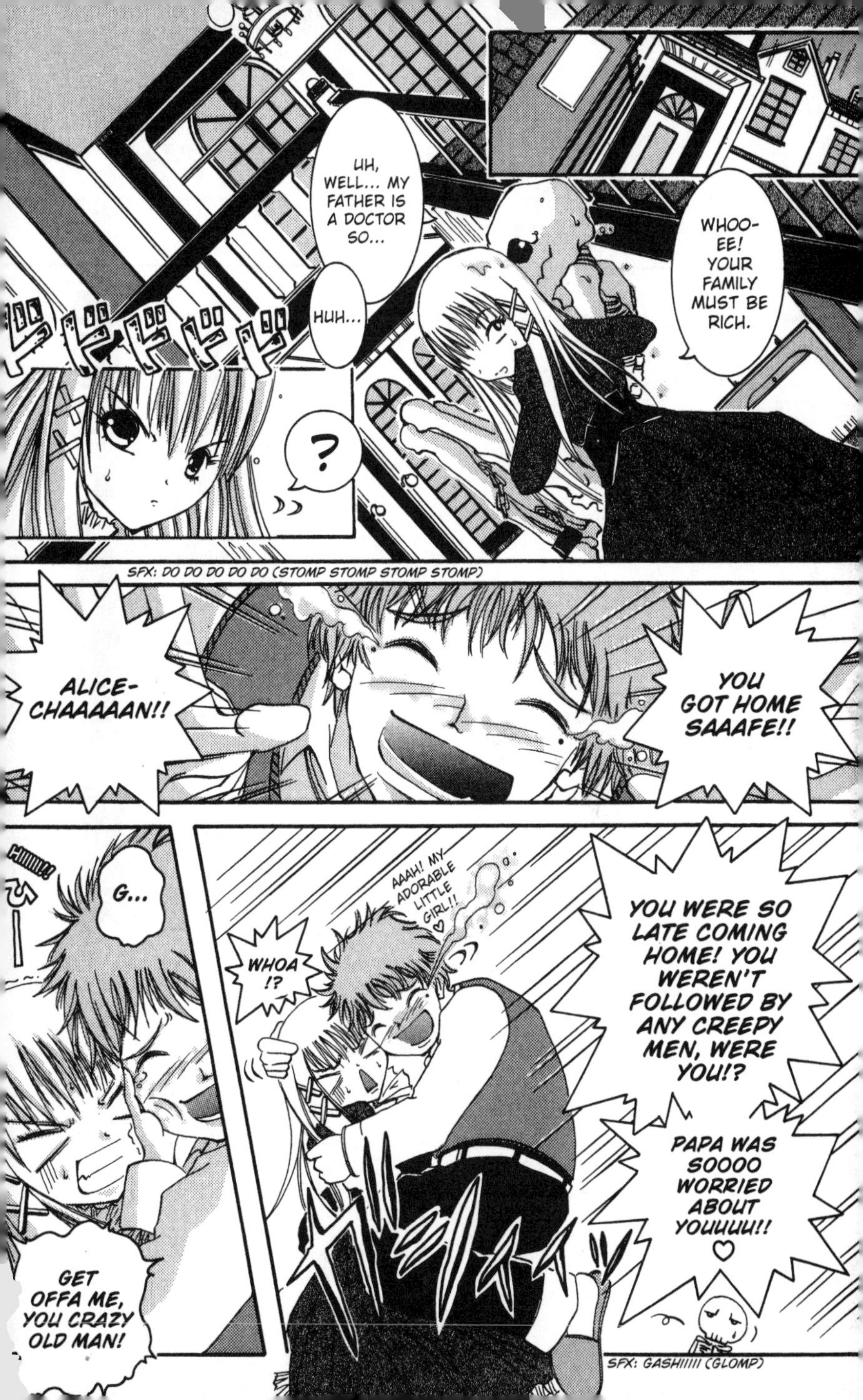
WHOOO-EE! YOUR FAMILY MUST BE RICH.
UH, WELL... MY FATHER IS A DOCTOR SO...
HUH...
?
SFX: DO DO DO DO DO (STOMP STOMP STOMP STOMP)
YOU GOT HOME SAAAFE!!
ALICE-CHAAAAAN!!
YOU WERE SO LATE COMING HOME! YOU WEREN'T FOLLOWED BY ANY CREEPY MEN, WERE YOU!?
PAPA WAS SOOOO WORRIED ABOUT YOUUUU!! ♥
AAAH! MY ADORABLE LITTLE GIRL!! ♥
WHOA !?
SFX: GASHIIIII (GLOMP)
G...
GET OFFA ME, YOU CRAZY OLD MAN!

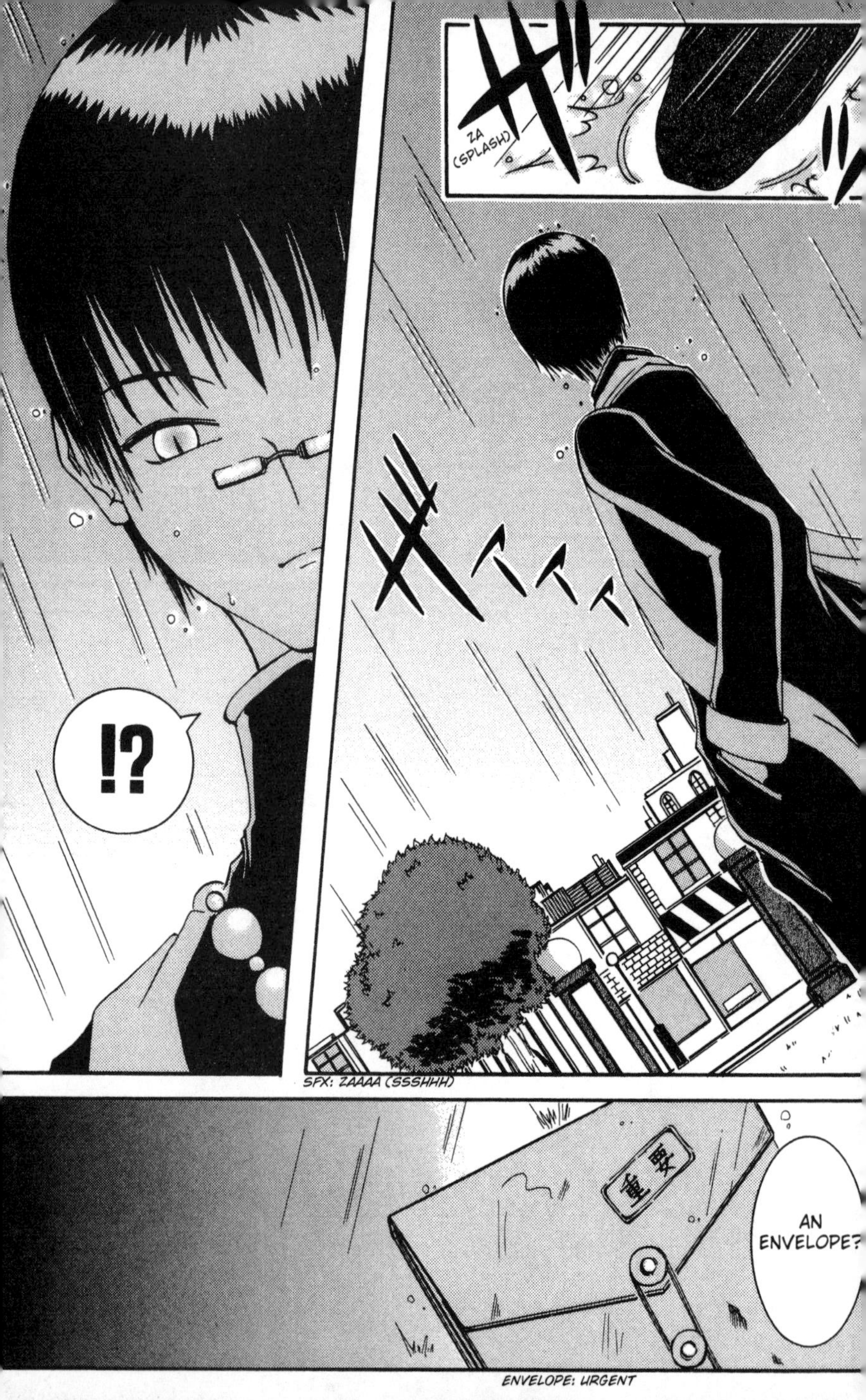
ZA (SPLASH)
SFX: ZAAAA (SSSHHH)
!?
AN ENVELOPE?
ENVELOPE: URGENT

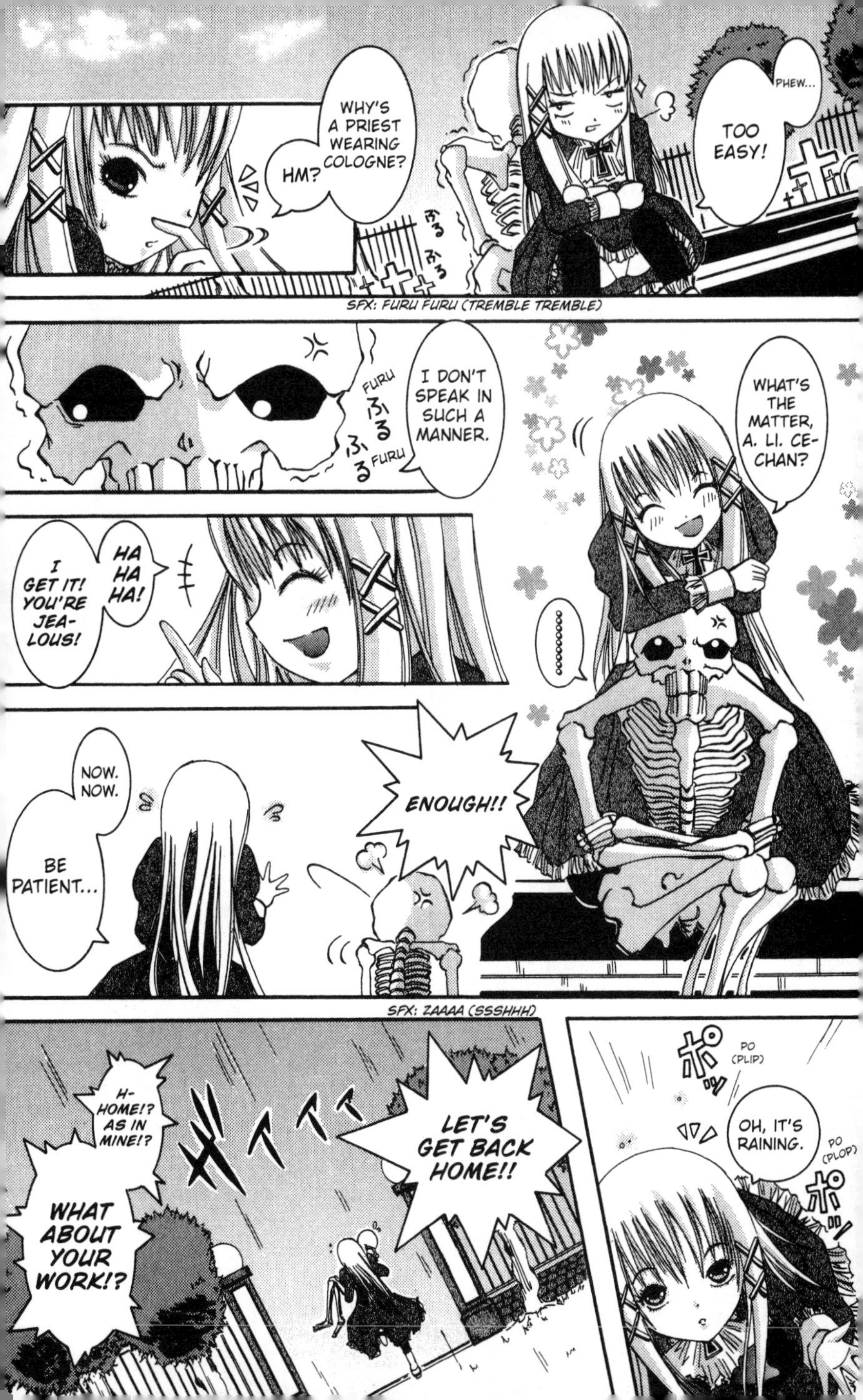

PHEW...
TOO EASY!
HM?
WHY'S A PRIEST WEARING COLOGNE?
ふる ふる
SFX: FURU FURU (TREMBLE TREMBLE)
WHAT'S THE MATTER, A. LI. CE-CHAN?
....
I DON'T SPEAK IN SUCH A MANNER.
FURU ふる ふる FURU
HA HA HA!
I GET IT! YOU'RE JEA-LOUS!
ENOUGH!!
NOW. NOW.
BE PATIENT...
SFX: ZAAAA (SSSHHH)
ポ PO (PLIP)
OH, IT'S RAINING.
PO (PLOP) ポ
LET'S GET BACK HOME!!
H-HOME!? AS IN MINE!?
WHAT ABOUT YOUR WORK!?

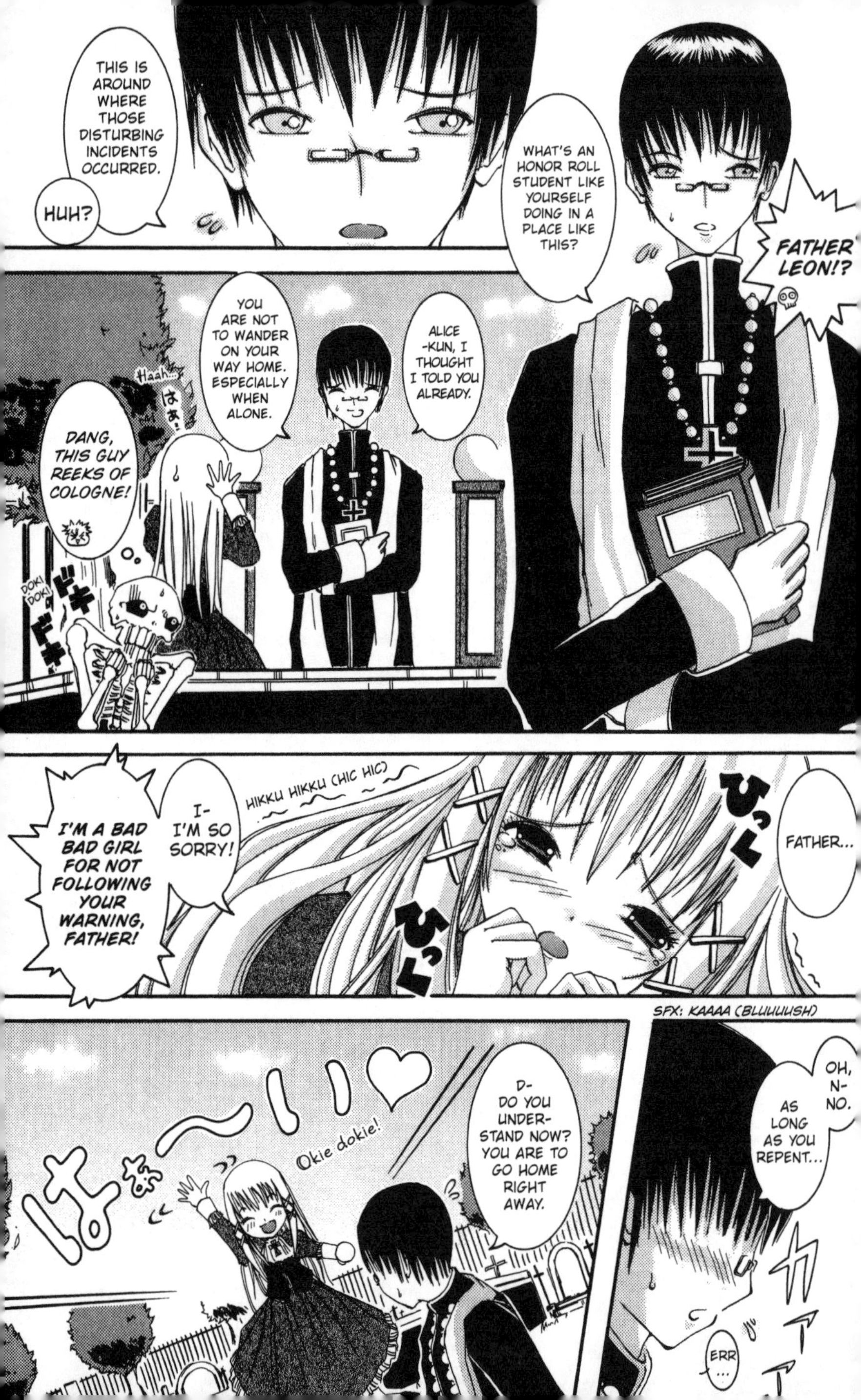
WHAT'S AN HONOR ROLL STUDENT LIKE YOURSELF DOING IN A PLACE LIKE THIS?
FATHER LEON!?
THIS IS AROUND WHERE THOSE DISTURBING INCIDENTS OCCURRED.
HUH?
ALICE -KUN, I THOUGHT I TOLD YOU ALREADY.
YOU ARE NOT TO WANDER ON YOUR WAY HOME. ESPECIALLY WHEN ALONE.
Haah... はぁ！
DANG, THIS GUY REEKS OF COLOGNE!
DOKI DOKI ドキドキ
FATHER...
ひっく ひっく
HIKKU HIKKU (HIC HIC)
I- I'M SO SORRY!
I'M A BAD BAD GIRL FOR NOT FOLLOWING YOUR WARNING, FATHER!
SFX: KAAAA (BLUUUUSH)
OH, N- NO.
AS LONG AS YOU REPENT...
カァァ
ERR ...
D- DO YOU UNDER- STAND NOW? YOU ARE TO GO HOME RIGHT AWAY.
はーい
Okie dokie!

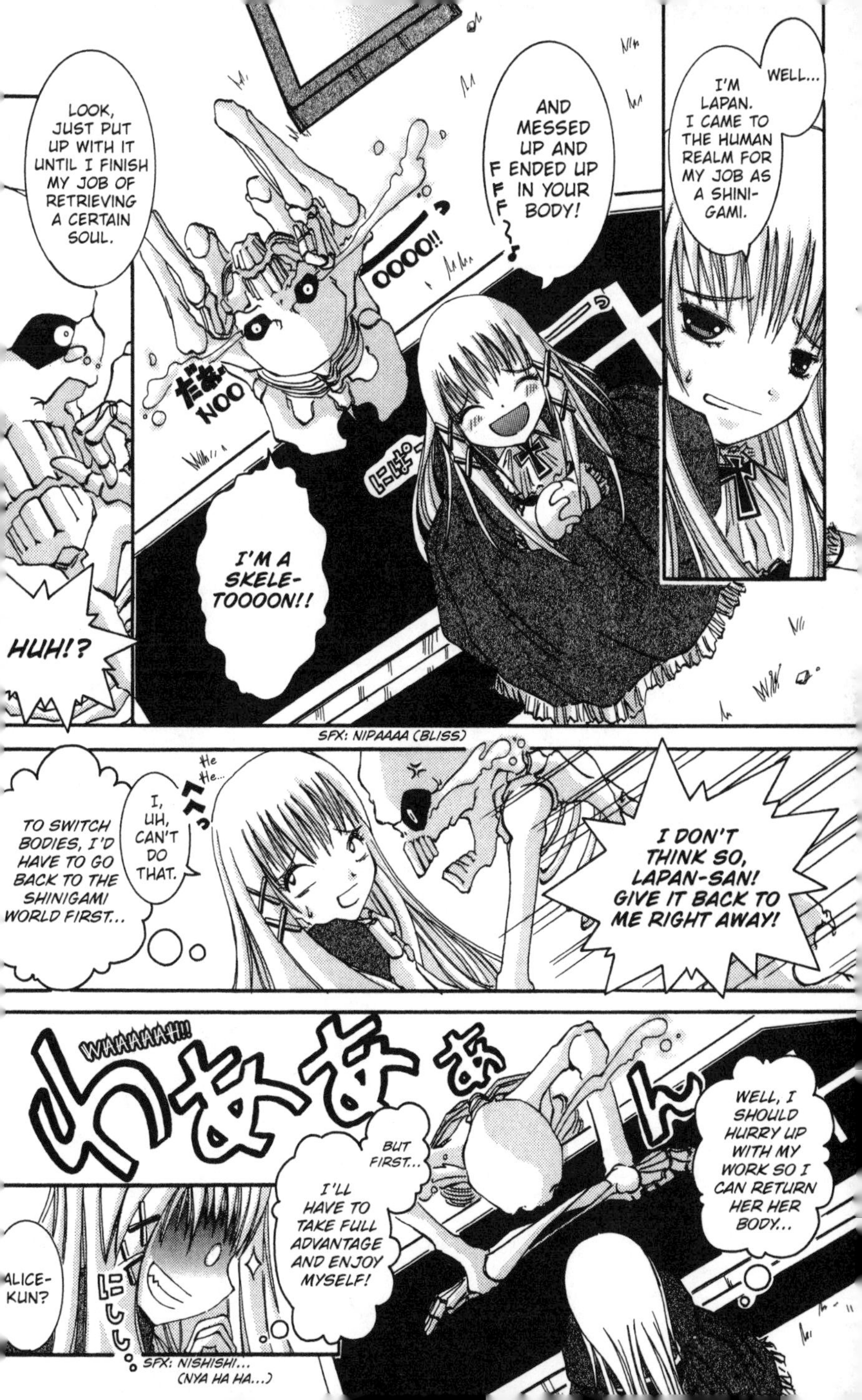
WELL...
I'M LAPAN. I CAME TO THE HUMAN REALM FOR MY JOB AS A SHINIGAMI.
AND MESSED UP AND ENDED UP IN YOUR BODY!
FFF~
—OOOO!!
NOO
I'M A SKELE-TOOOON!!
LOOK, JUST PUT UP WITH IT UNTIL I FINISH MY JOB OF RETRIEVING A CERTAIN SOUL.
HUH!?
SFX: NIPAAAA (BLISS)
I DON'T THINK SO, LAPAN-SAN! GIVE IT BACK TO ME RIGHT AWAY!
He He...
I, UH, CAN'T DO THAT.
TO SWITCH BODIES, I'D HAVE TO GO BACK TO THE SHINIGAMI WORLD FIRST...
WAAAAAAH!!
WELL, I SHOULD HURRY UP WITH MY WORK SO I CAN RETURN HER HER BODY...
BUT FIRST...
I'LL HAVE TO TAKE FULL ADVANTAGE AND ENJOY MYSELF!
ALICE-KUN?
SFX: NISHISHI... (NYA HA HA...)

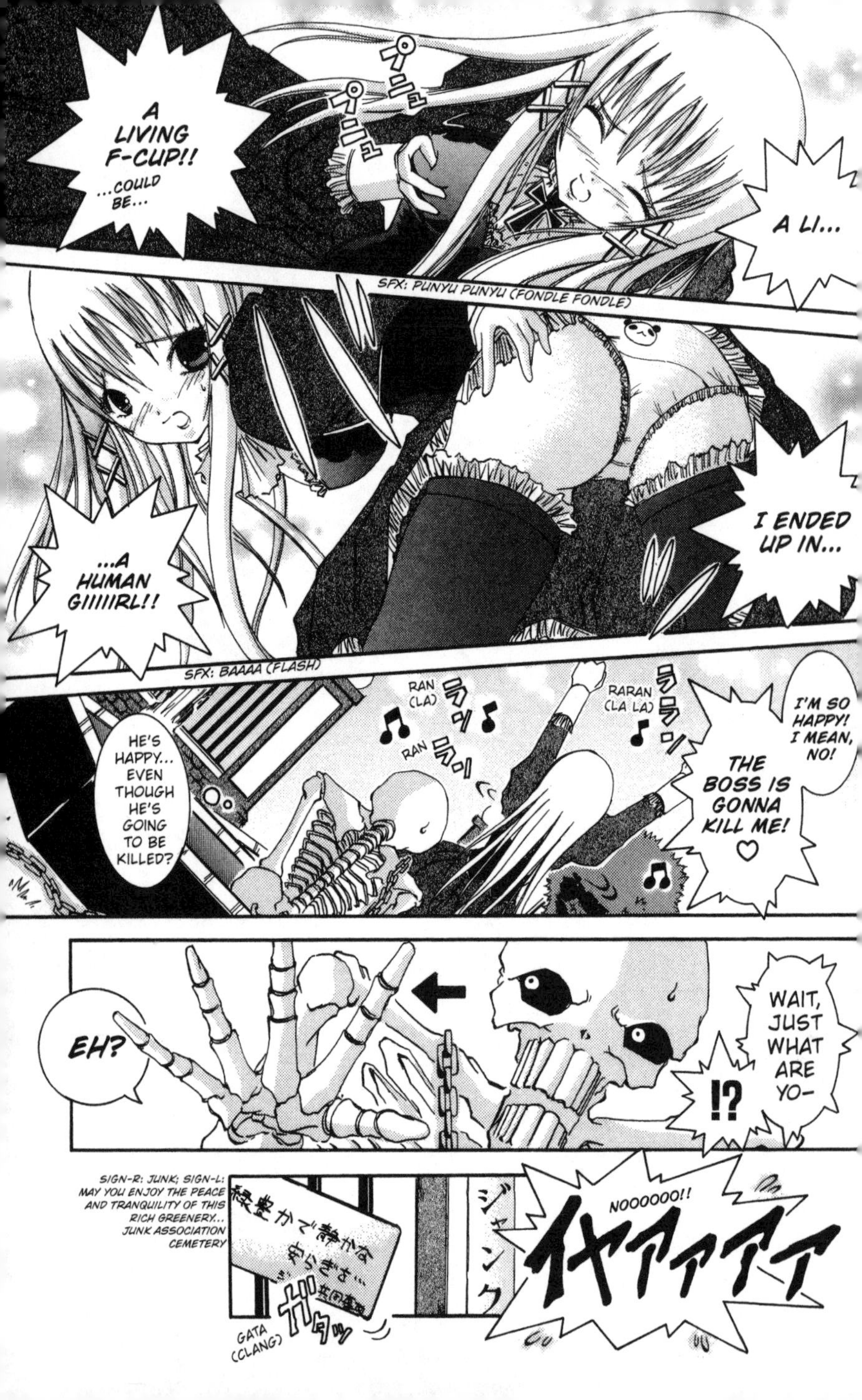
A LI...
A LIVING F-CUP!! ...COULD BE...
SFX: PUNYU PUNYU (FONDLE FONDLE)
I ENDED UP IN...
...A HUMAN GIIIIIRL!!
SFX: BAAAA (FLASH)
I'M SO HAPPY! I MEAN, NO!
THE BOSS IS GONNA KILL ME! ♡
RARAN (LA LA)
RAN (LA)
RAN
HE'S HAPPY... EVEN THOUGH HE'S GOING TO BE KILLED?
WAIT, JUST WHAT ARE YO-
!?
EH?
NOOOOOO!!
ジャンク
SIGN-R: JUNK; SIGN-L: MAY YOU ENJOY THE PEACE AND TRANQUILITY OF THIS RICH GREENERY... JUNK ASSOCIATION CEMETERY
GATA (CLANG)

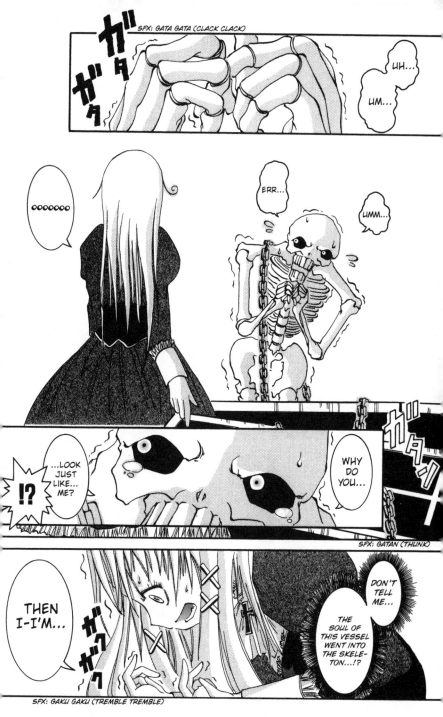

SFX: GATA GATA (CLACK CLACK)

UH...

UM...

ooooooo

ERR...

UMM...

!?

...LOOK JUST LIKE... ME?

WHY DO YOU...

SFX: GATAN (THUNK)

THEN I-I'M...

DON'T TELL ME...

THE SOUL OF THIS VESSEL WENT INTO THE SKELE-TON...!?

SFX: GAKU GAKU (TREMBLE TREMBLE)

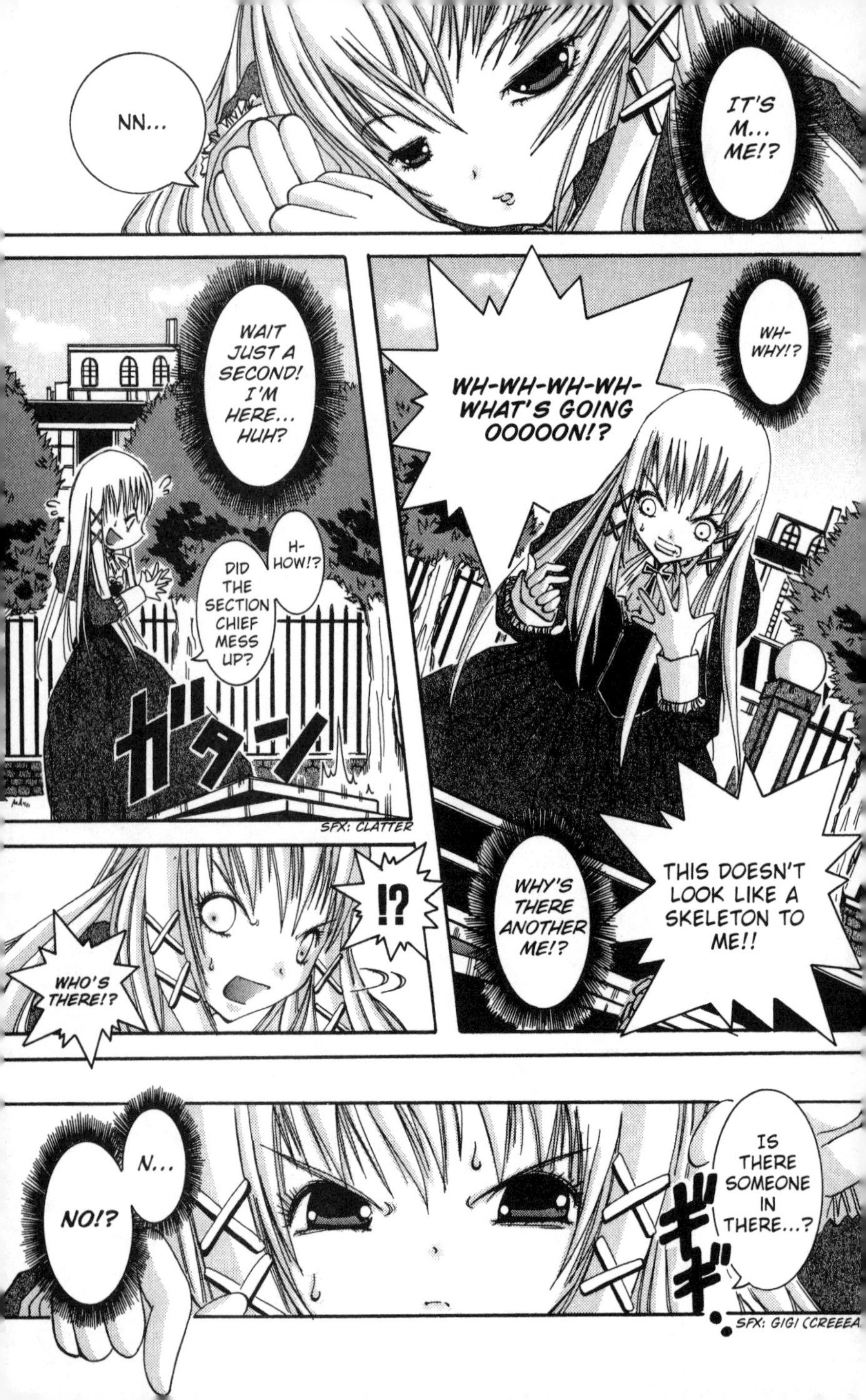
IT'S M... ME!?
NN...
WH- WHY!?
WH-WH-WH-WH-WHAT'S GOING OOOOON!?
THIS DOESN'T LOOK LIKE A SKELETON TO ME!!
WHY'S THERE ANOTHER ME!?
WAIT JUST A SECOND! I'M HERE... HUH?
H- HOW!?
DID THE SECTION CHIEF MESS UP?
SFX: CLATTER
!?
WHO'S THERE!?
IS THERE SOMEONE IN THERE...?
SFX: GIGI (CREEEA
N...
NO!?

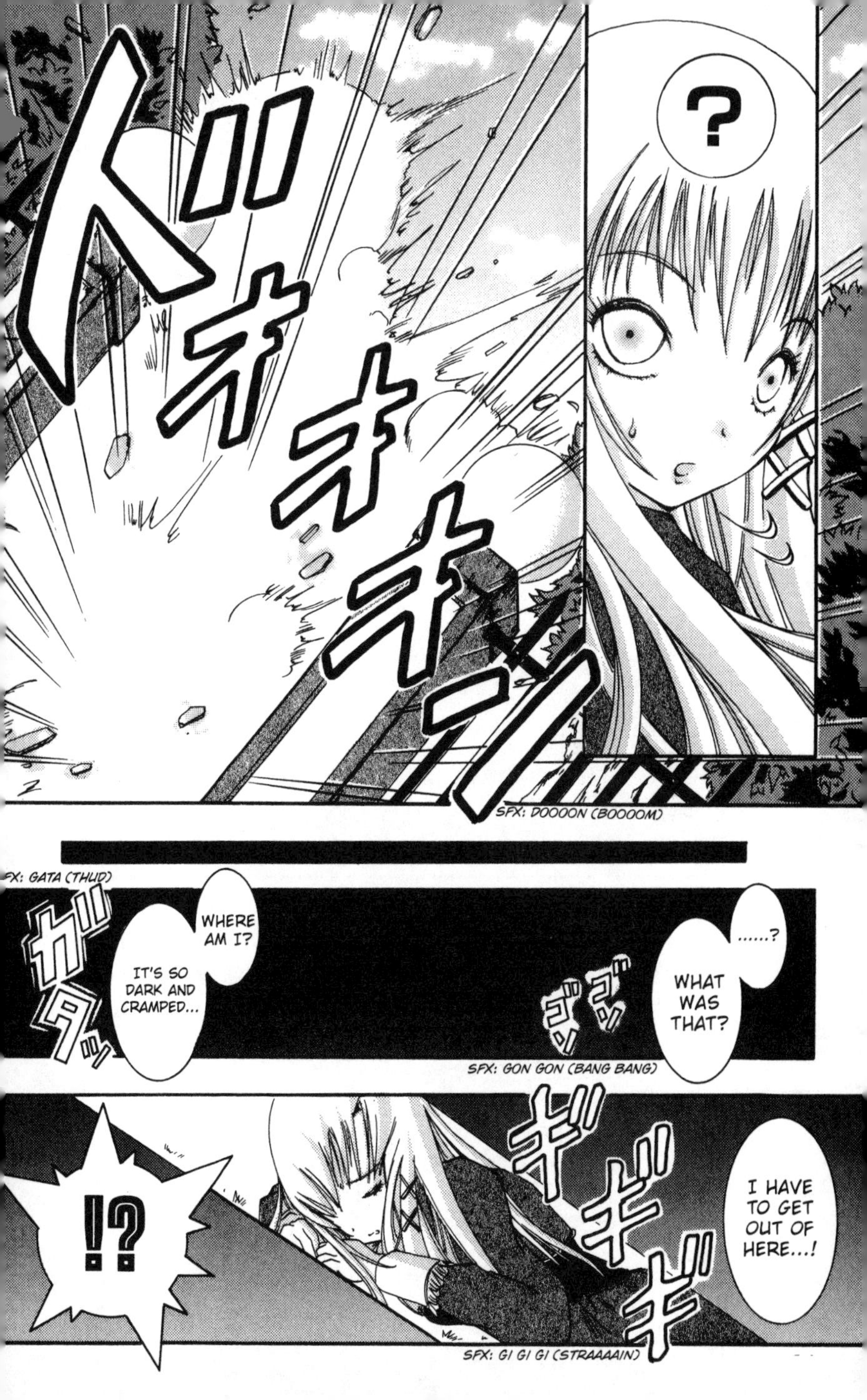
?
SFX: DOOOON (BOOOOM)
......?
WHAT WAS THAT?
SFX: GON GON (BANG BANG)
WHERE AM I?
IT'S SO DARK AND CRAMPED...
FX: GATA (THUD)
I HAVE TO GET OUT OF HERE...!
SFX: GI GI GI (STRAAAAIN)
!?

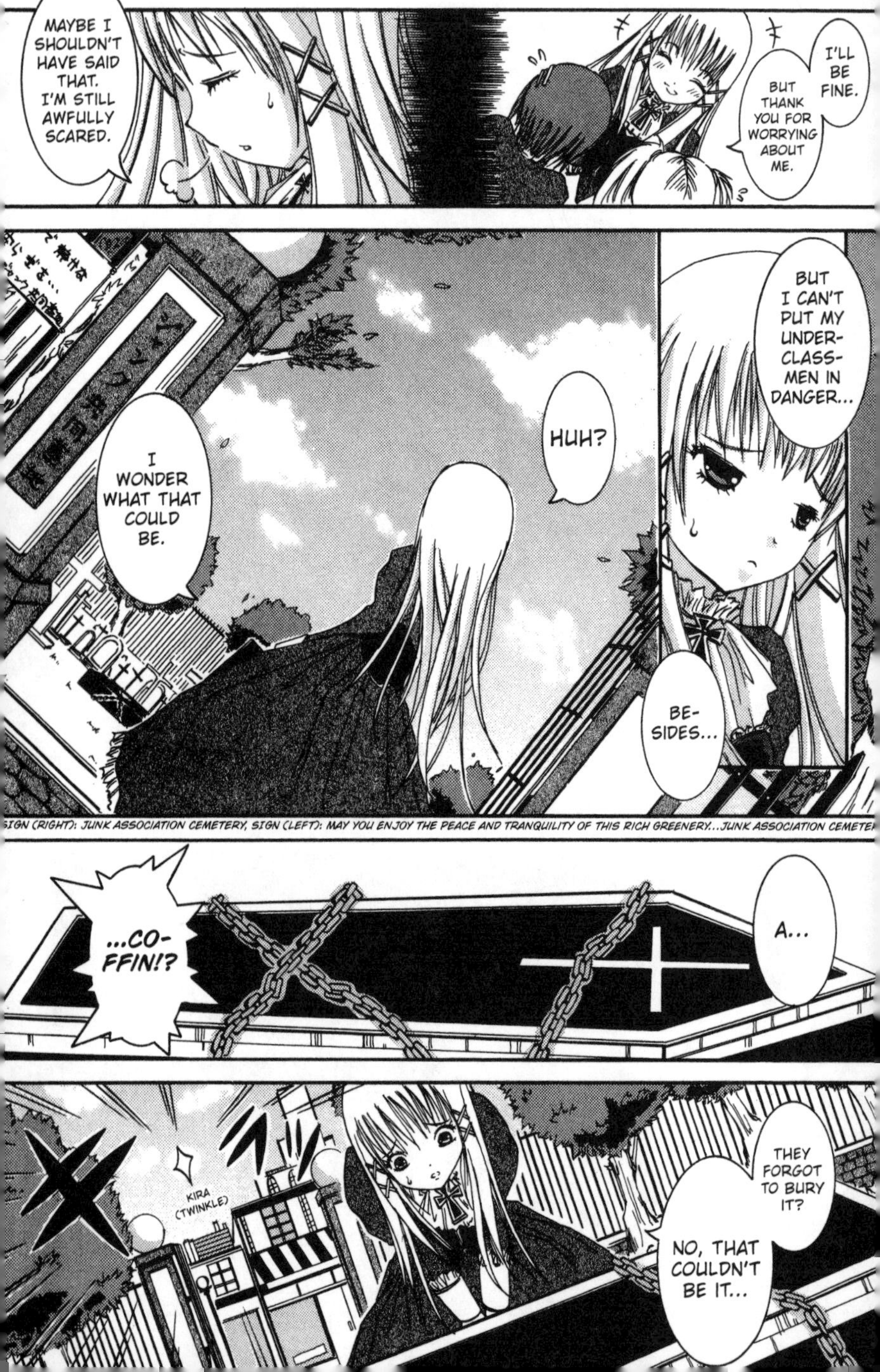
I'LL BE FINE.
BUT THANK YOU FOR WORRYING ABOUT ME.
MAYBE I SHOULDN'T HAVE SAID THAT. I'M STILL AWFULLY SCARED.
BUT I CAN'T PUT MY UNDER-CLASS-MEN IN DANGER...
BE-SIDES...
HUH?
I WONDER WHAT THAT COULD BE.
SIGN (RIGHT): JUNK ASSOCIATION CEMETERY, SIGN (LEFT): MAY YOU ENJOY THE PEACE AND TRANQUILITY OF THIS RICH GREENERY...JUNK ASSOCIATION CEMETE
A...
...CO-FFIN!?
THEY FORGOT TO BURY IT?
NO, THAT COULDN'T BE IT...
KIRA (TWINKLE)

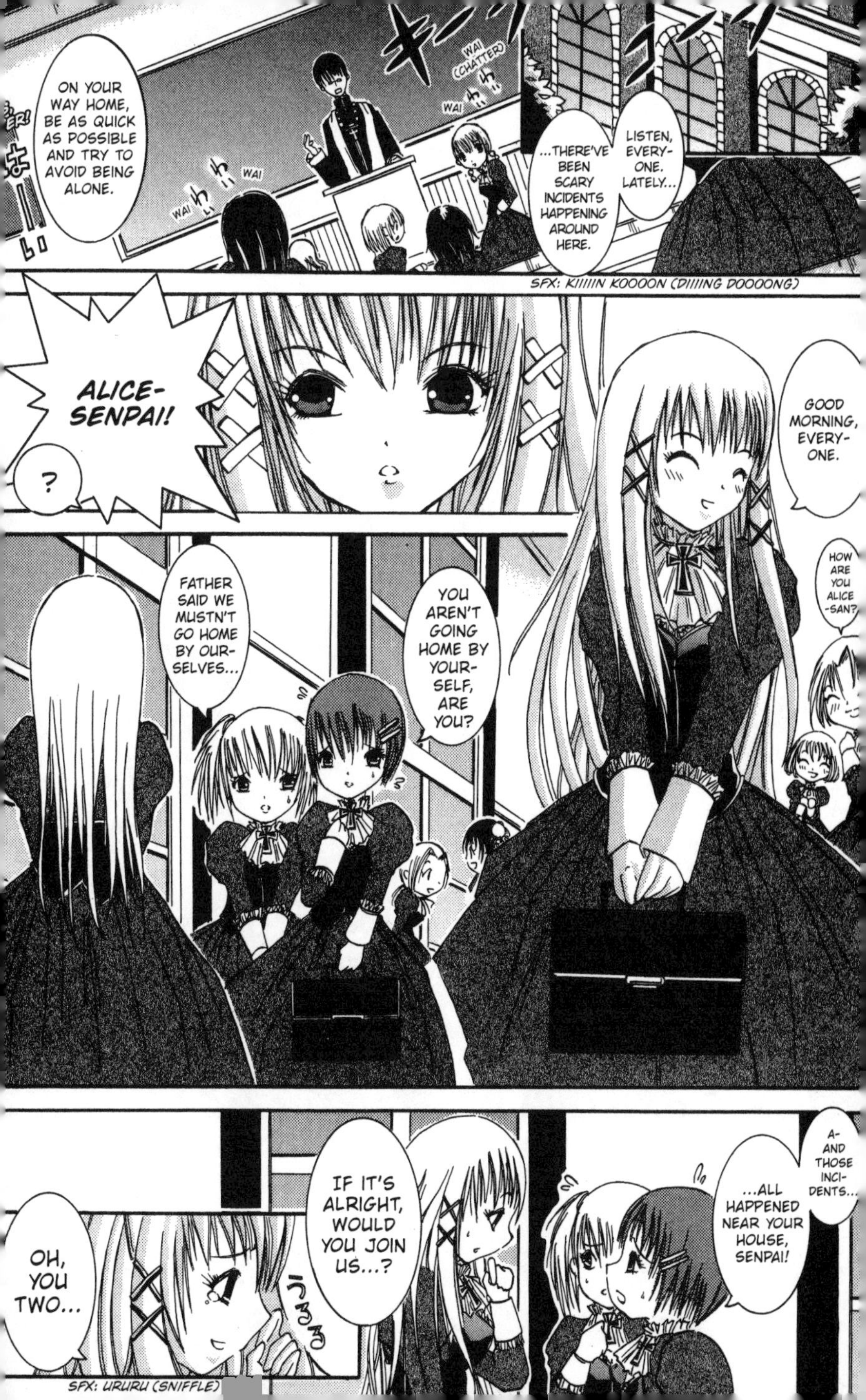

LISTEN, EVERY-ONE. LATELY...
...THERE'VE BEEN SCARY INCIDENTS HAPPENING AROUND HERE.
WAI (CHATTER)
WAI
WAI
WAI
ON YOUR WAY HOME, BE AS QUICK AS POSSIBLE AND TRY TO AVOID BEING ALONE.
SFX: KIIIIIN KOOOON (DIIIING DOOOONG)
GOOD MORNING, EVERY-ONE.
HOW ARE YOU ALICE-SAN?
ALICE-SENPAI!
?
YOU AREN'T GOING HOME BY YOUR-SELF, ARE YOU?
FATHER SAID WE MUSTN'T GO HOME BY OUR-SELVES...
A- AND THOSE INCI-DENTS...
...ALL HAPPENED NEAR YOUR HOUSE, SENPAI!
IF IT'S ALRIGHT, WOULD YOU JOIN US...?
OH, YOU TWO...
SFX: URURU (SNIFFLE)

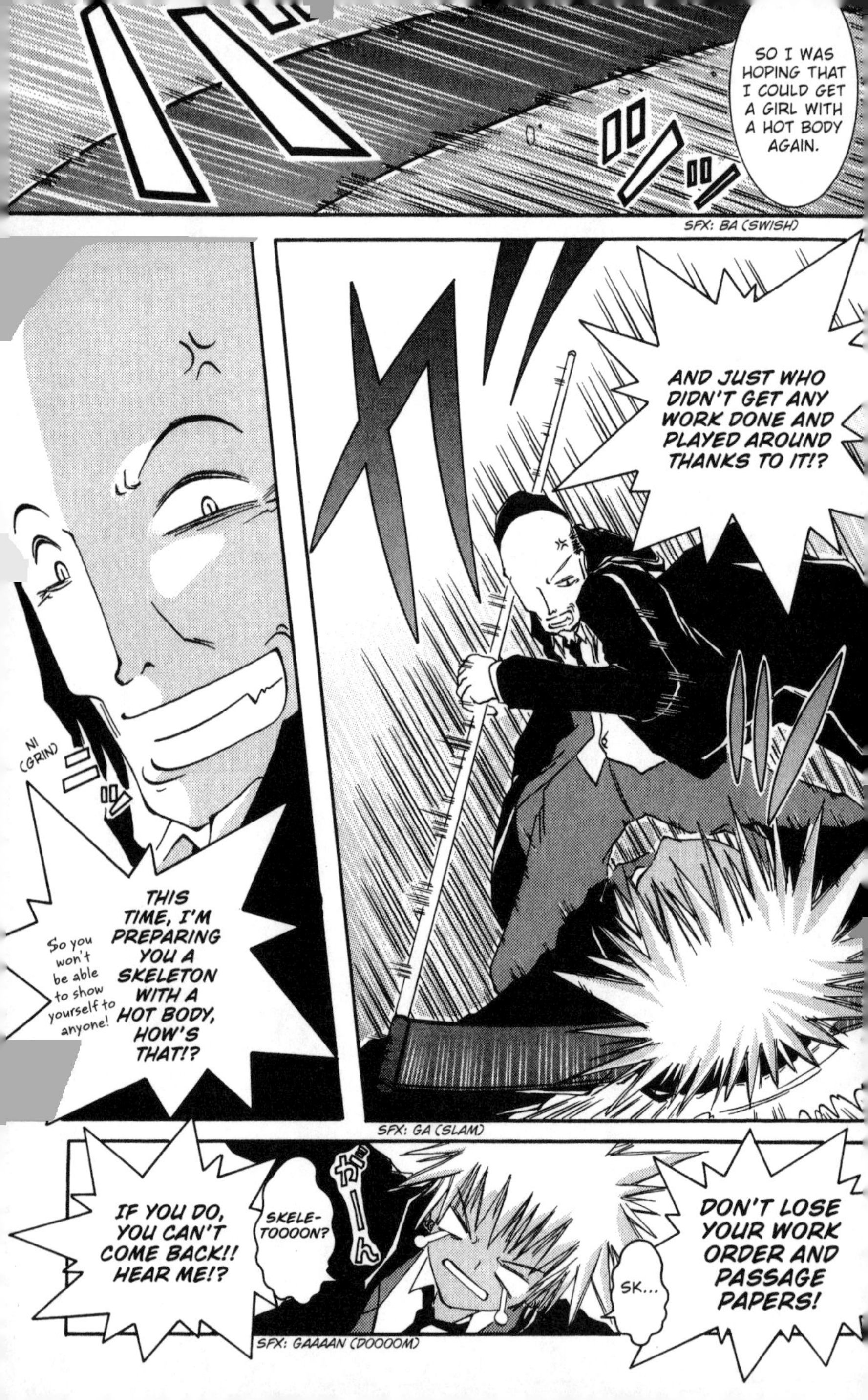
SO I WAS HOPING THAT I COULD GET A GIRL WITH A HOT BODY AGAIN.
SFX: BA (SWISH)
AND JUST WHO DIDN'T GET ANY WORK DONE AND PLAYED AROUND THANKS TO IT!?
SFX: GA (SLAM)
NI (GRIN)
THIS TIME, I'M PREPARING YOU A SKELETON WITH A HOT BODY, HOW'S THAT!?
So you won't be able to show yourself to anyone!
DON'T LOSE YOUR WORK ORDER AND PASSAGE PAPERS!
SK...
SKELE-TOOOON?
IF YOU DO, YOU CAN'T COME BACK!! HEAR ME!?
SFX: GAAAAN (DOOOOM)

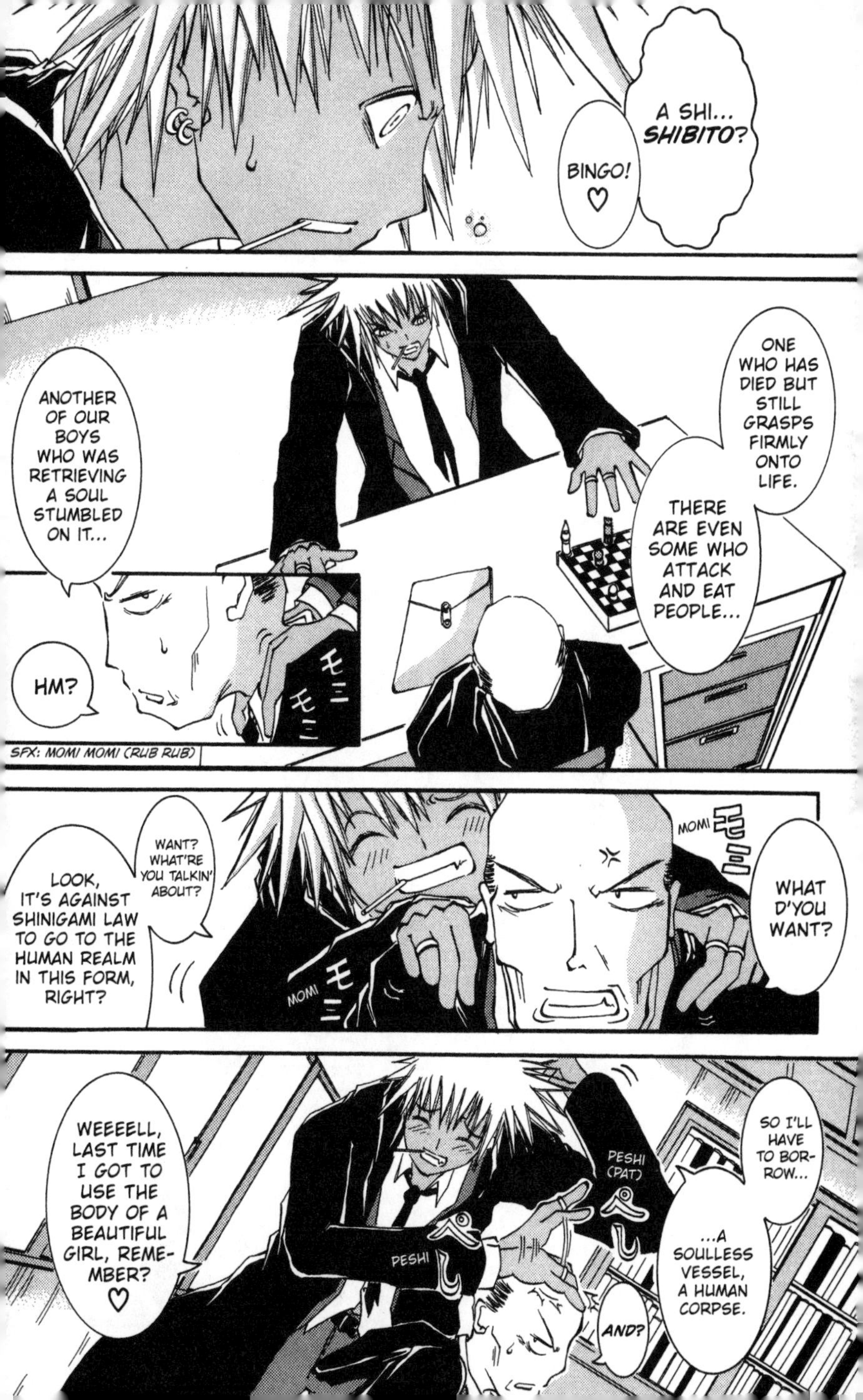
A SHI... SHIBITO?
BINGO! ♡
ONE WHO HAS DIED BUT STILL GRASPS FIRMLY ONTO LIFE.
THERE ARE EVEN SOME WHO ATTACK AND EAT PEOPLE...
ANOTHER OF OUR BOYS WHO WAS RETRIEVING A SOUL STUMBLED ON IT...
HM?
SFX: MOMI MOMI (RUB RUB)
MOMI
WHAT D'YOU WANT?
WANT? WHAT'RE YOU TALKIN' ABOUT?
LOOK, IT'S AGAINST SHINIGAMI LAW TO GO TO THE HUMAN REALM IN THIS FORM, RIGHT?
MOMI
SO I'LL HAVE TO BORROW...
...A SOULLESS VESSEL, A HUMAN CORPSE.
PESHI (PAT)
PESHI
AND?
WEEEELL, LAST TIME I GOT TO USE THE BODY OF A BEAUTIFUL GIRL, REMEMBER? ♡

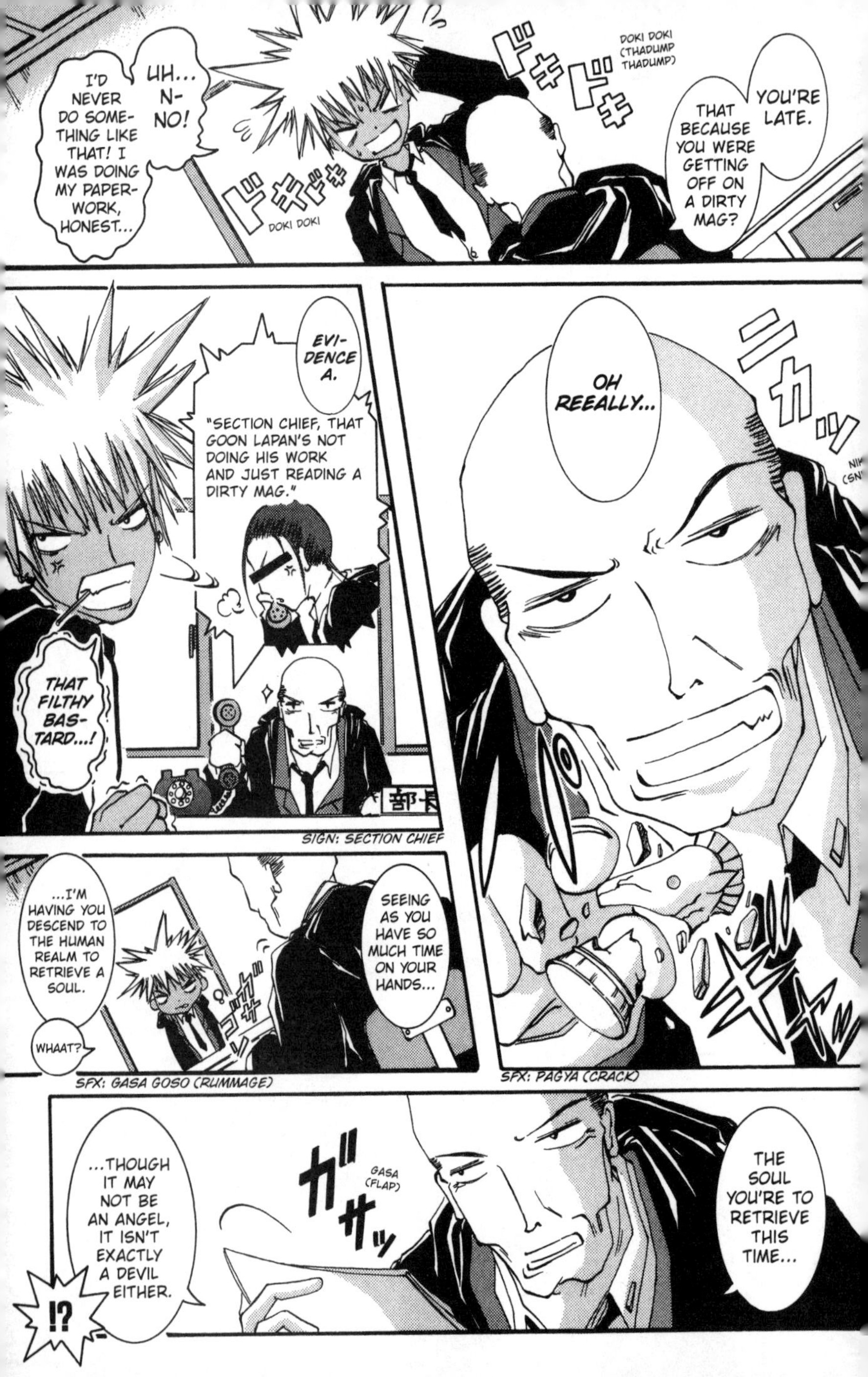
DOKI DOKI (THADUMP THADUMP)
YOU'RE LATE.
THAT BECAUSE YOU WERE GETTING OFF ON A DIRTY MAG?
UH... N-NO!
I'D NEVER DO SOMETHING LIKE THAT! I WAS DOING MY PAPERWORK, HONEST...
DOKI DOKI
OH REEALLY...
SFX: PAGYA (CRACK)
EVIDENCE A.
"SECTION CHIEF, THAT GOON LAPAN'S NOT DOING HIS WORK AND JUST READING A DIRTY MAG."
THAT FILTHY BASTARD...!
部長
SIGN: SECTION CHIEF
SEEING AS YOU HAVE SO MUCH TIME ON YOUR HANDS...
...I'M HAVING YOU DESCEND TO THE HUMAN REALM TO RETRIEVE A SOUL.
WHAAT?
SFX: GASA GOSO (RUMMAGE)
THE SOUL YOU'RE TO RETRIEVE THIS TIME...
GASA (FLAP)
...THOUGH IT MAY NOT BE AN ANGEL, IT ISN'T EXACTLY A DEVIL EITHER.
!?

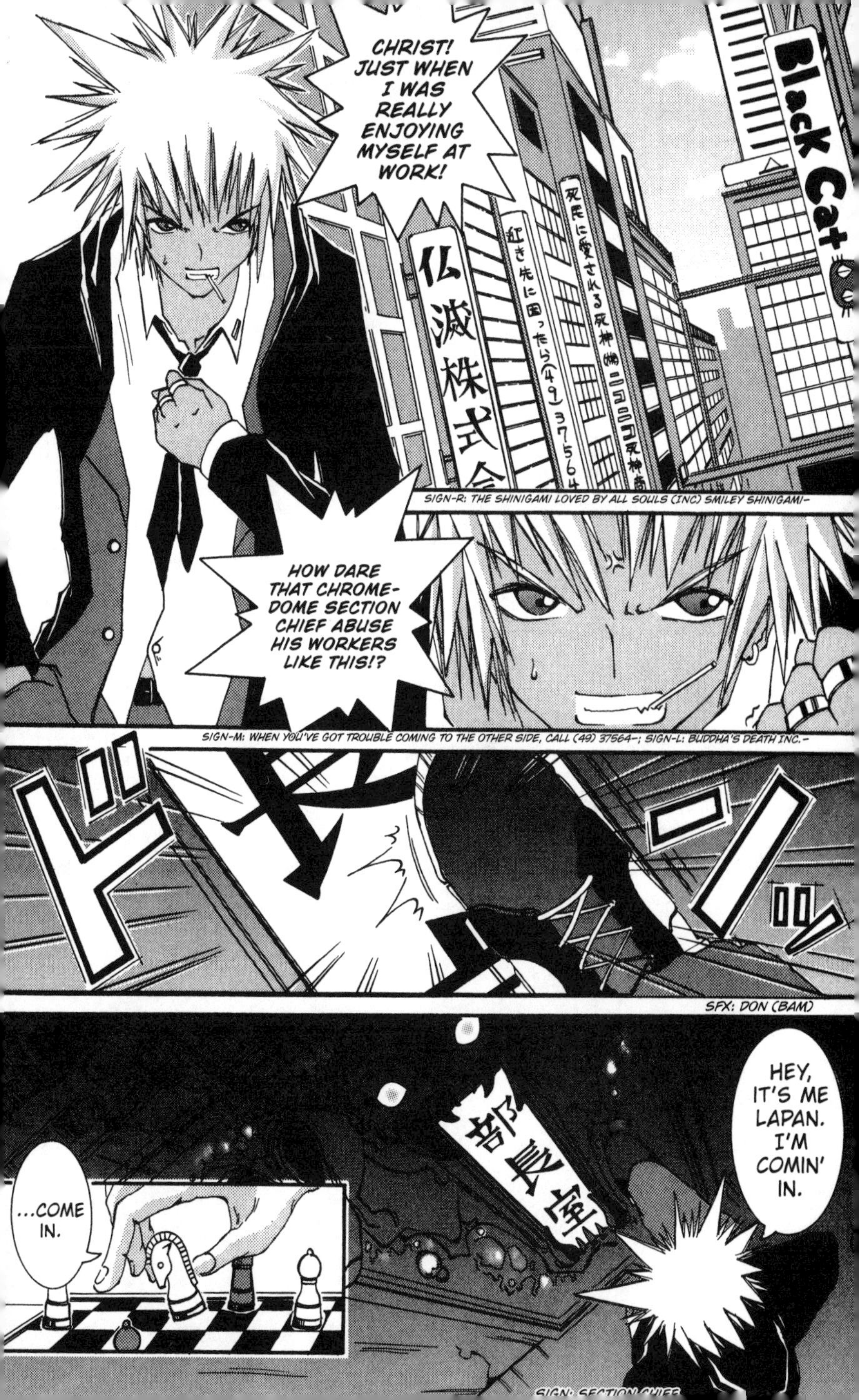
CHRIST! JUST WHEN I WAS REALLY ENJOYING MYSELF AT WORK!
Black Cat
死民に愛される死神㈱ニコニコ死神商
近き先に困ったら(49)37564
仏滅株式会
SIGN-R: THE SHINIGAMI LOVED BY ALL SOULS (INC) SMILEY SHINIGAMI-
HOW DARE THAT CHROME-DOME SECTION CHIEF ABUSE HIS WORKERS LIKE THIS!?
SIGN-M: WHEN YOU'VE GOT TROUBLE COMING TO THE OTHER SIDE, CALL (49) 37564-; SIGN-L: BUDDHA'S DEATH INC.-
ドーン
SFX: DON (BAM)
HEY, IT'S ME LAPAN. I'M COMIN' IN.
部長室
...COME IN.

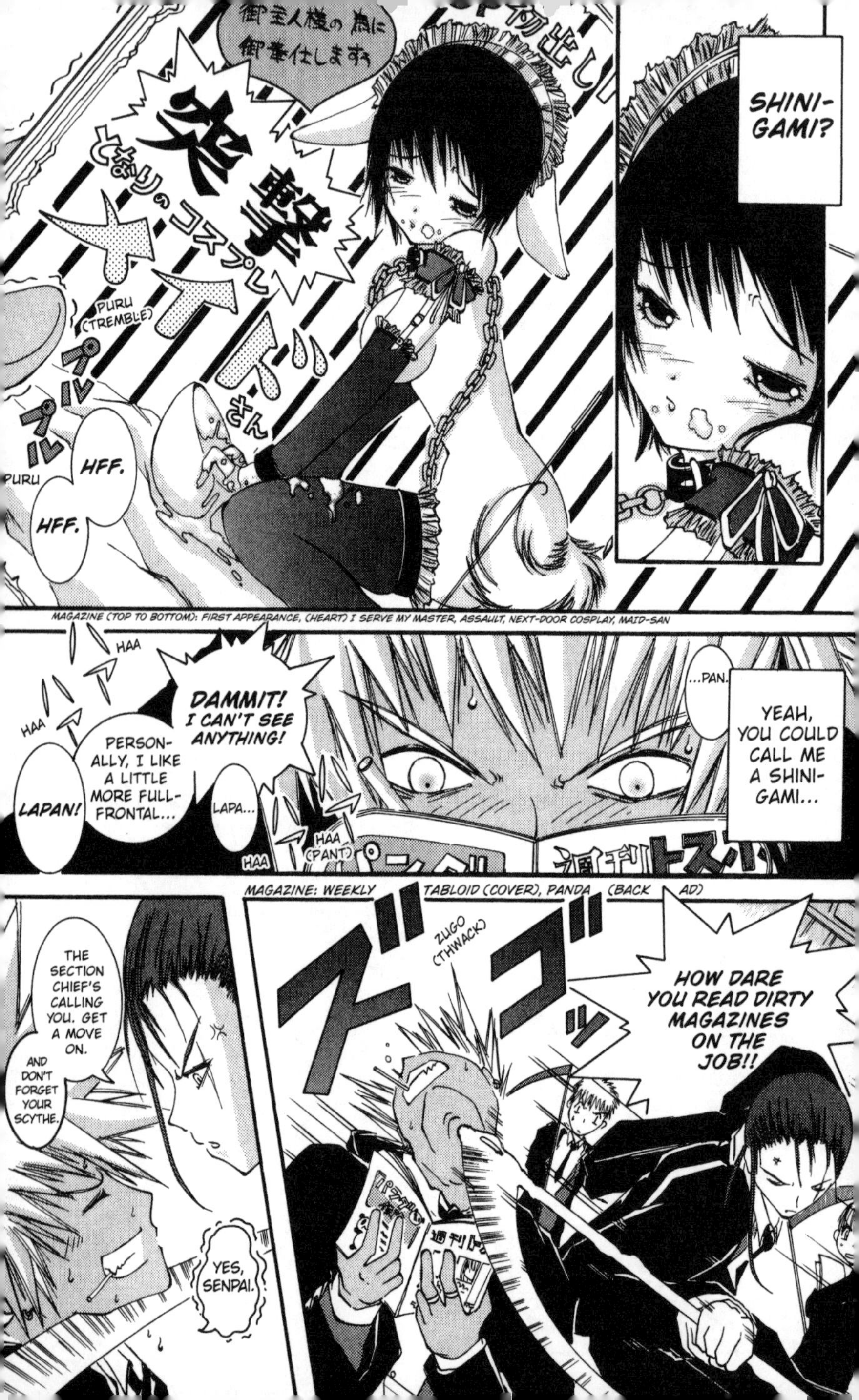
SHINI-GAMI?
御主人様の為に御奉仕します♪
突撃
となりのコスプレ
メイドさん
PURU (TREMBLE)
プルプル
PURU
HFF.
HFF.
MAGAZINE (TOP TO BOTTOM): FIRST APPEARANCE, (HEART) I SERVE MY MASTER, ASSAULT, NEXT-DOOR COSPLAY, MAID-SAN
YEAH, YOU COULD CALL ME A SHINI-GAMI...
...PAN.
DAMMIT! I CAN'T SEE ANYTHING!
LAPA...
PERSONALLY, I LIKE A LITTLE MORE FULL-FRONTAL...
LAPAN!
HAA
HAA
HAA (PANT)
HAA
MAGAZINE: WEEKLY TABLOID (COVER), PANDA (BACK AD)
HOW DARE YOU READ DIRTY MAGAZINES ON THE JOB!!
ZUGO (THWACK)
THE SECTION CHIEF'S CALLING YOU. GET A MOVE ON.
AND DON'T FORGET YOUR SCYTHE.
YES, SENPAI.

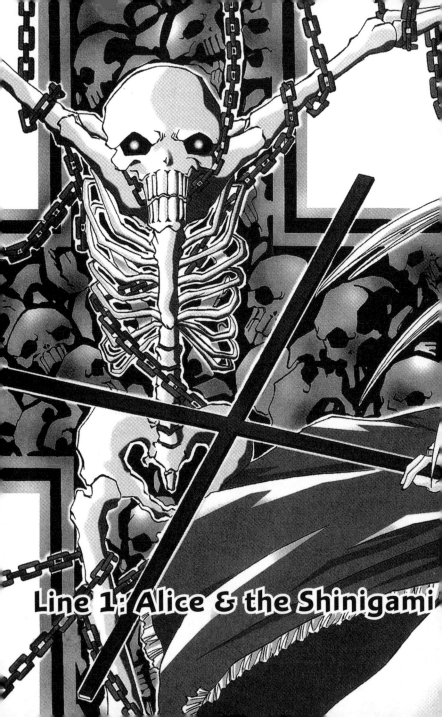

Line 1: Alice & the Shinigami

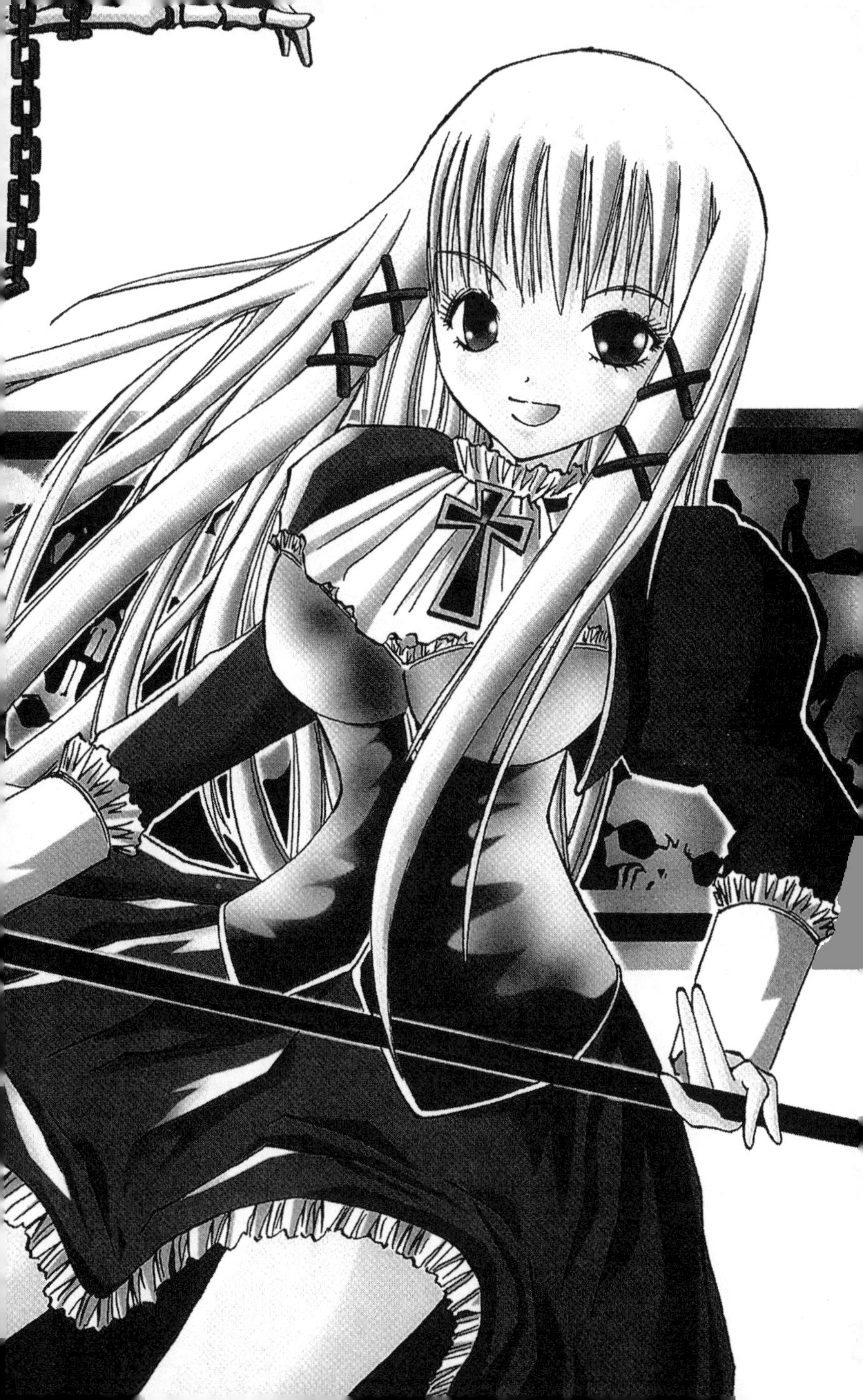

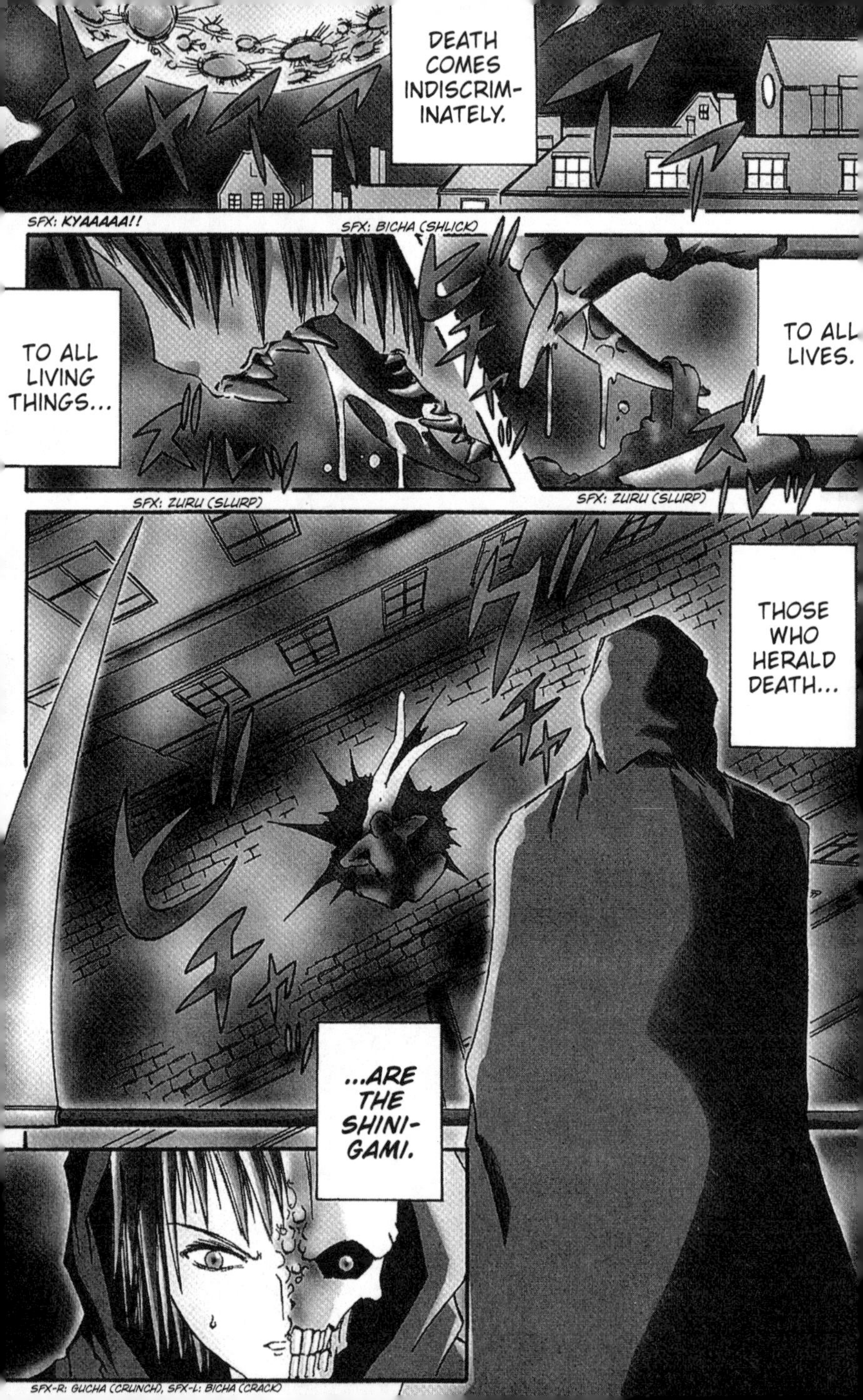
DEATH COMES INDISCRIMINATELY.
SFX: BICHA (SHLICK)
SFX: KYAAAAA!!
TO ALL LIVES.
SFX: ZURU (SLURP)
TO ALL LIVING THINGS...
SFX: ZURU (SLURP)
THOSE WHO HERALD DEATH...
...ARE THE SHINIGAMI.
SFX-R: GUCHA (CRUNCH), SFX-L: BICHA (CRACK)

ALICE ON DEADLINES

D線上のアリス

As punishment for slacking on the job, the shinigami Lapan is ordered to go to the Human Realm in the body of a skeleton to retrieve a wandering soul. However, much to Lapan's lecherous delight, a slip-up lands his soul in the body of the young Alice, a buxom student at a local all-girls' school. With the skirt-chasing shinigami (as Alice) leaving a storm of sexual harassment allegations in his wake, whatever is poor, beskeletoned Alice to do?!

Poor schoolgirl Alice discovers that angels of death are anything but angelic!

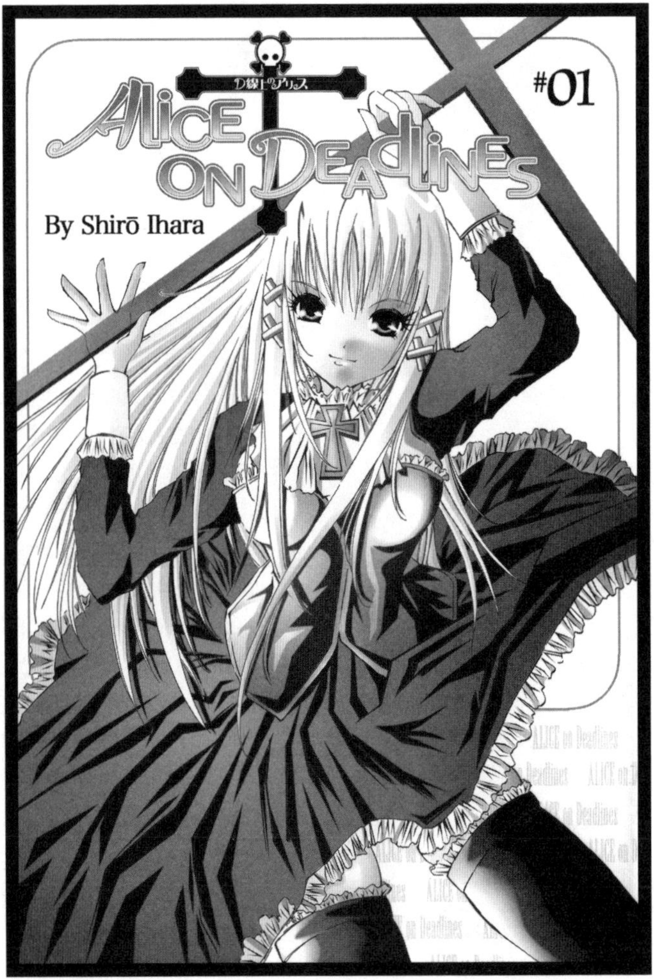
D線上のアリス
ALICE ON DEADLINES
#01
By Shirō Ihara

OLDER TEEN OT LNSV

- ISBN-13: 978-0-7595-2351-7
- ISBN-10: 0-7595-2351-7
- $10.99 USD/$12.75 CAN/£5.99 UK
- November 2007

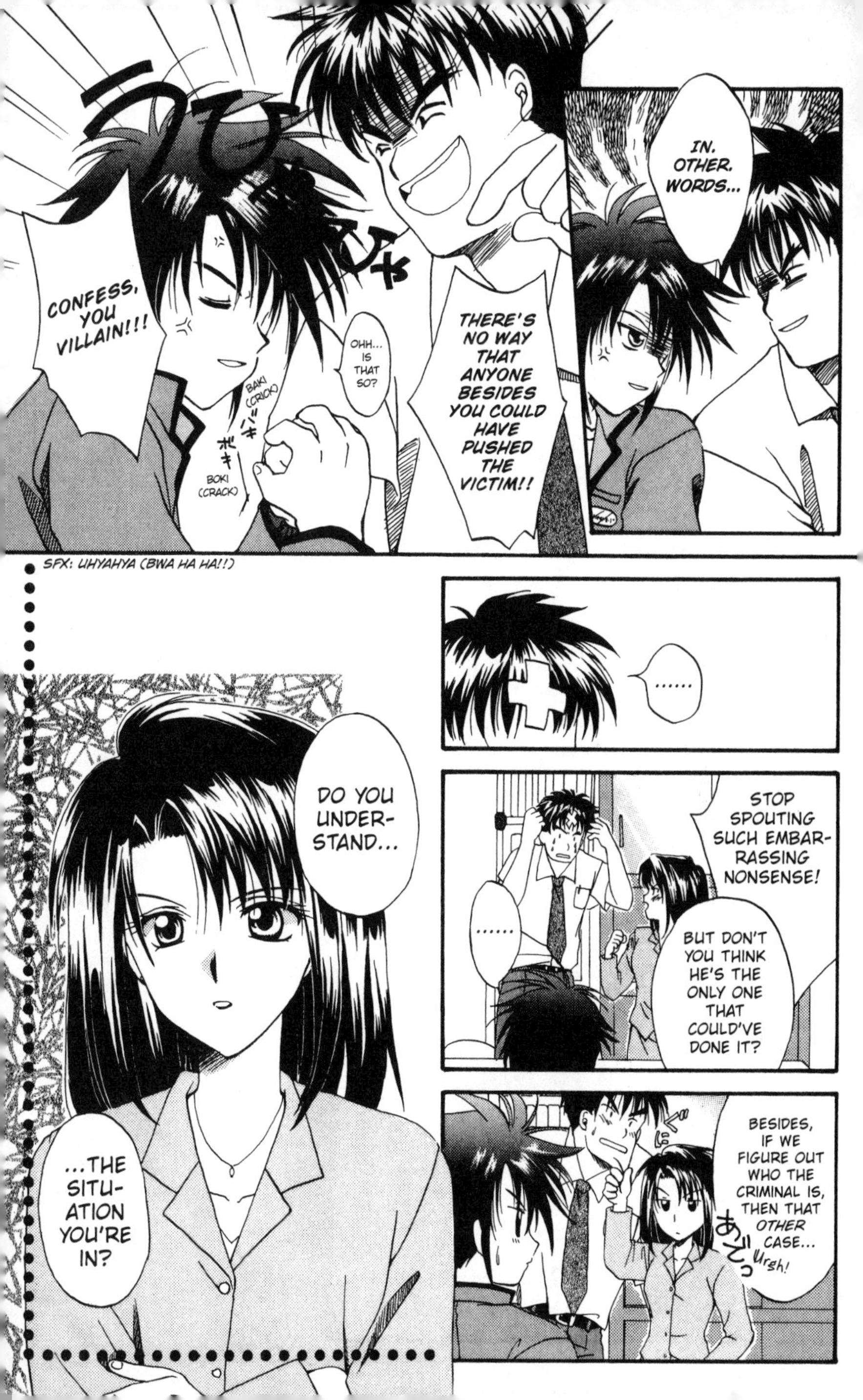
IN. OTHER. WORDS...
THERE'S NO WAY THAT ANYONE BESIDES YOU COULD HAVE PUSHED THE VICTIM!!
OHH... IS THAT SO?
BAKI (CRICK)
BOKI (CRACK)
CONFESS, YOU VILLAIN!!!
SFX: UHYAHYA (BWA HA HA!!)
......
STOP SPOUTING SUCH EMBARRASSING NONSENSE!
......
BUT DON'T YOU THINK HE'S THE ONLY ONE THAT COULD'VE DONE IT?
BESIDES, IF WE FIGURE OUT WHO THE CRIMINAL IS, THEN THAT OTHER CASE...
Urgh!
DO YOU UNDERSTAND...
...THE SITUATION YOU'RE IN?

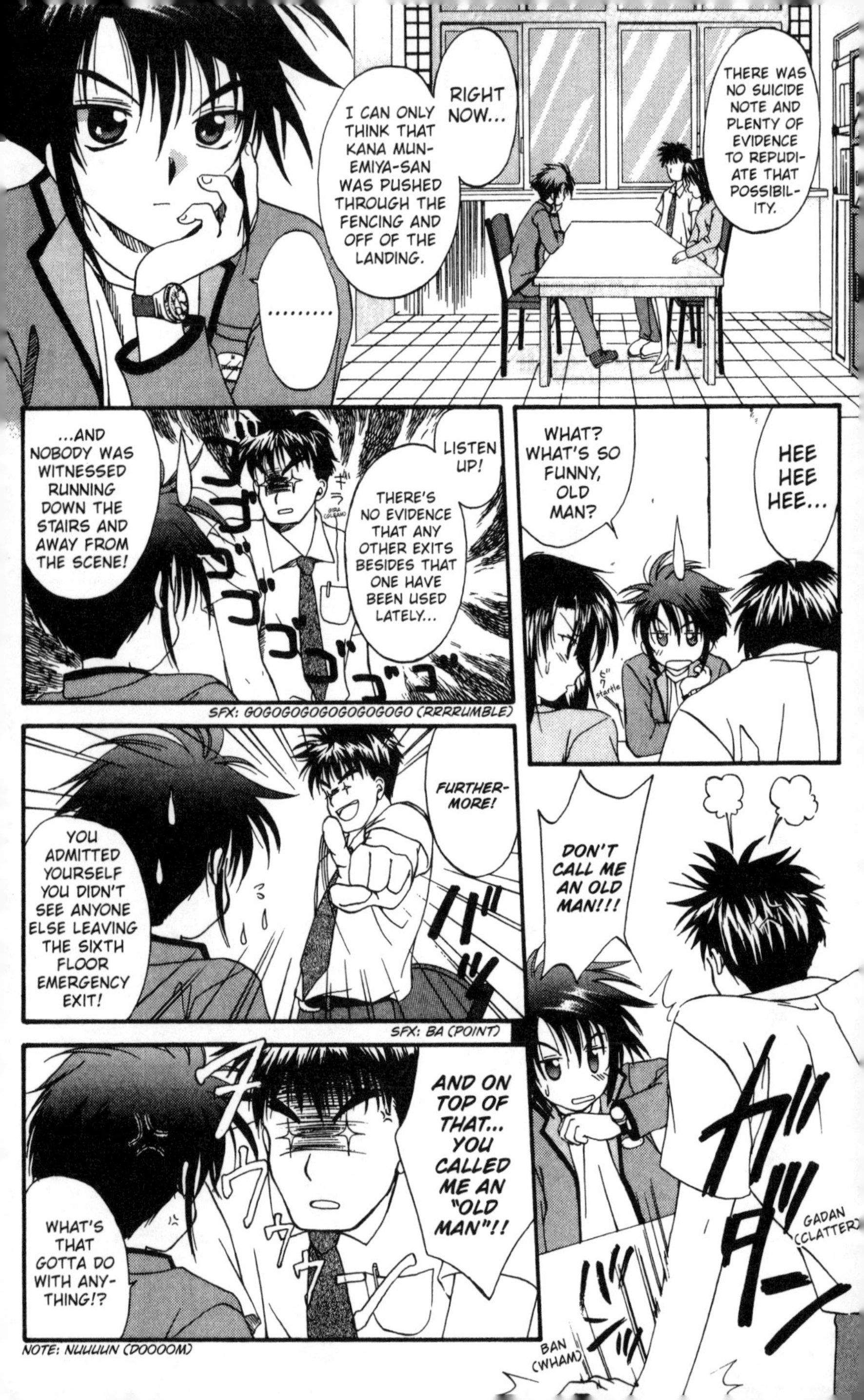
THERE WAS NO SUICIDE NOTE AND PLENTY OF EVIDENCE TO REPUDIATE THAT POSSIBILITY.
RIGHT NOW...
I CAN ONLY THINK THAT KANA MUNEMIYA-SAN WAS PUSHED THROUGH THE FENCING AND OFF OF THE LANDING.
....
HEE HEE HEE...
WHAT? WHAT'S SO FUNNY, OLD MAN?
startle
LISTEN UP!
GIRA (GLEAM)
THERE'S NO EVIDENCE THAT ANY OTHER EXITS BESIDES THAT ONE HAVE BEEN USED LATELY...
...AND NOBODY WAS WITNESSED RUNNING DOWN THE STAIRS AND AWAY FROM THE SCENE!
SFX: GOGOGOGOGOGOGOGOGO (RRRRUMBLE)
DON'T CALL ME AN OLD MAN!!!
GADAN (CLATTER)
BAN (WHAM)
FURTHERMORE!
YOU ADMITTED YOURSELF YOU DIDN'T SEE ANYONE ELSE LEAVING THE SIXTH FLOOR EMERGENCY EXIT!
SFX: BA (POINT)
AND ON TOP OF THAT... YOU CALLED ME AN "OLD MAN"!!
WHAT'S THAT GOTTA DO WITH ANYTHING!?
NOTE: NUUUUN (DOOOOM)

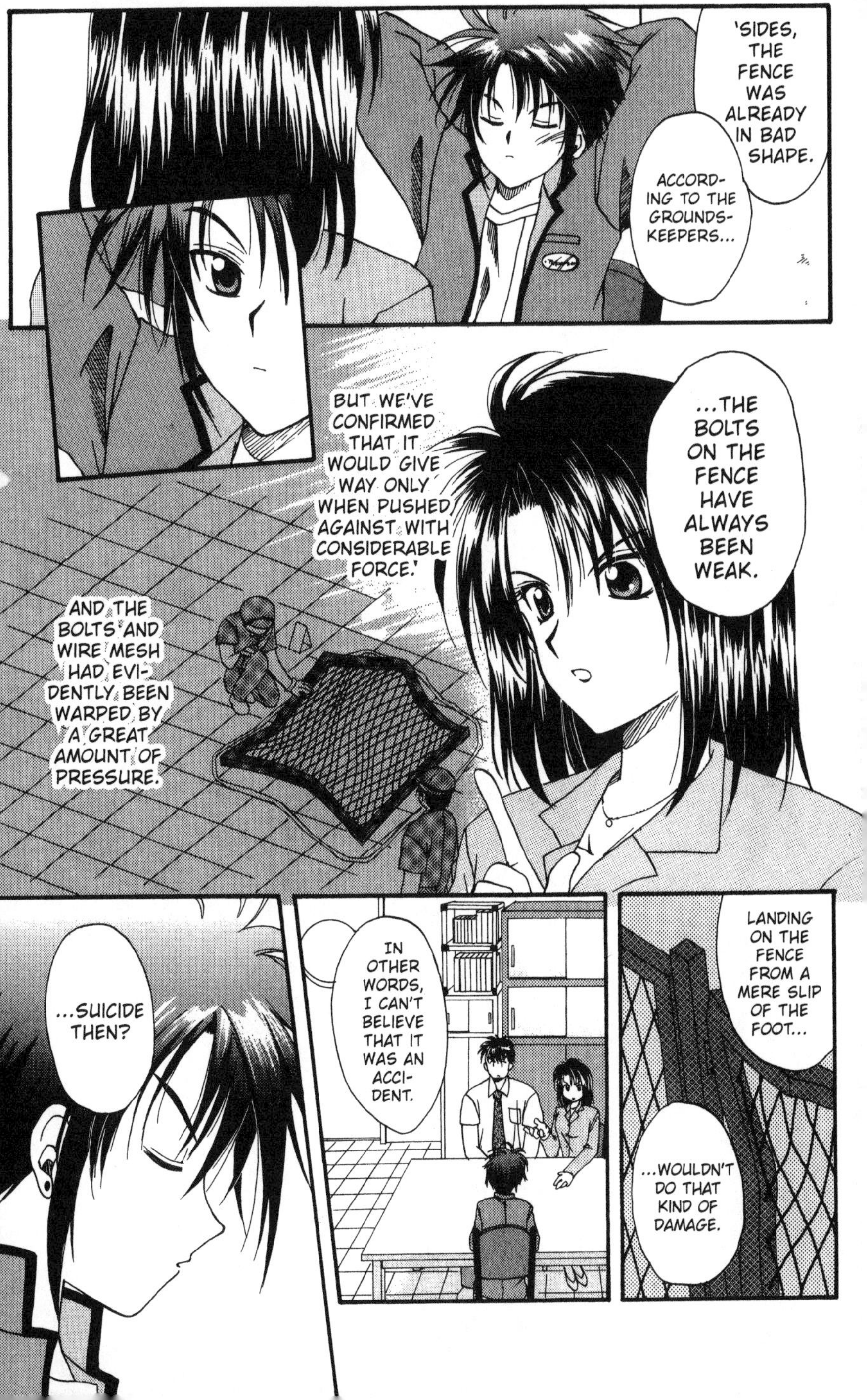
'SIDES, THE FENCE WAS ALREADY IN BAD SHAPE.
ACCORDING TO THE GROUNDSKEEPERS...
...THE BOLTS ON THE FENCE HAVE ALWAYS BEEN WEAK.
BUT WE'VE CONFIRMED THAT IT WOULD GIVE WAY ONLY WHEN PUSHED AGAINST WITH CONSIDERABLE FORCE.'
AND THE BOLTS AND WIRE MESH HAD EVIDENTLY BEEN WARPED BY A GREAT AMOUNT OF PRESSURE.
LANDING ON THE FENCE FROM A MERE SLIP OF THE FOOT...
...WOULDN'T DO THAT KIND OF DAMAGE.
IN OTHER WORDS, I CAN'T BELIEVE THAT IT WAS AN ACCIDENT.
...SUICIDE THEN?

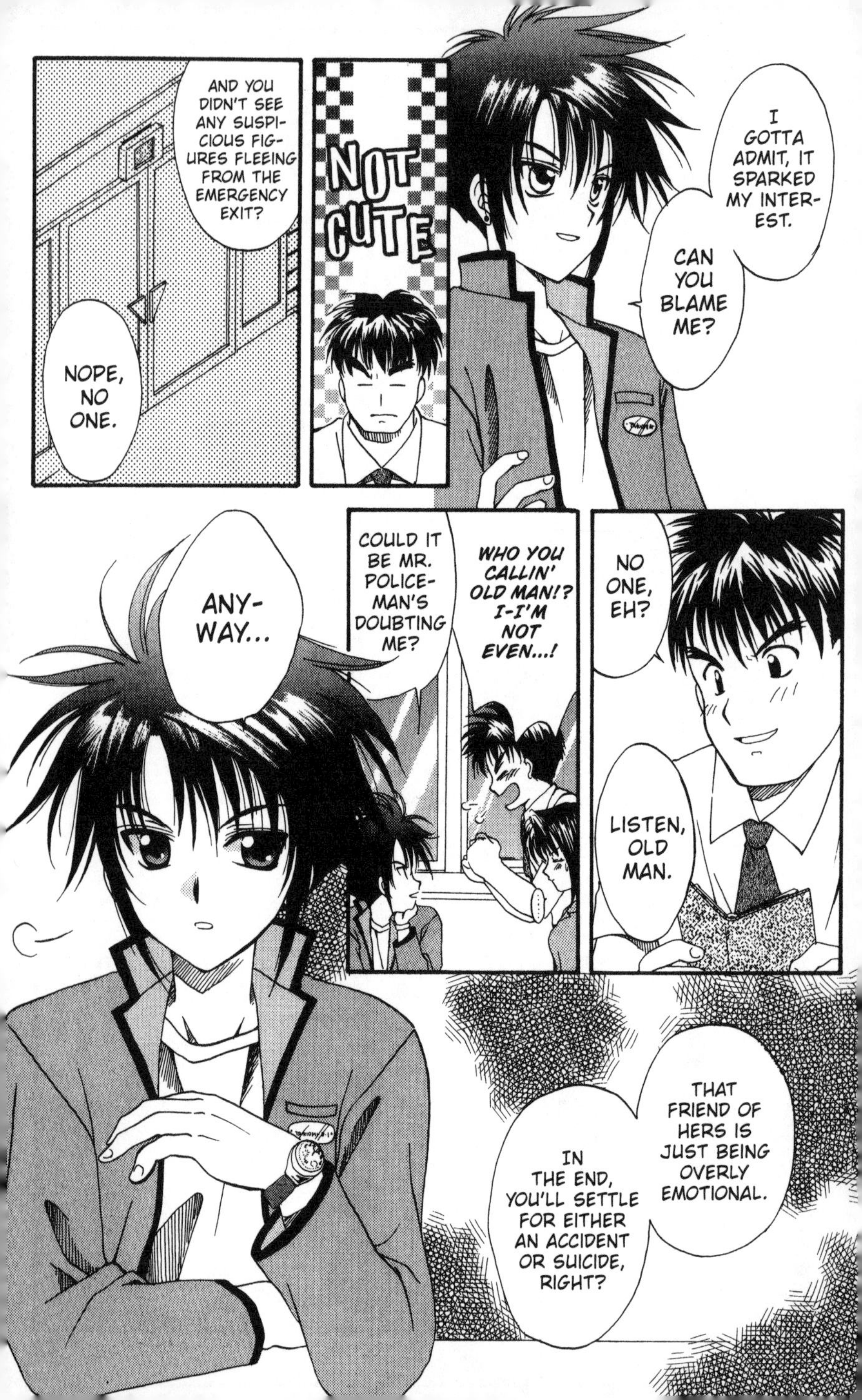
I GOTTA ADMIT, IT SPARKED MY INTER- EST.
CAN YOU BLAME ME?
NOT CUTE
AND YOU DIDN'T SEE ANY SUSPI- CIOUS FIG- URES FLEEING FROM THE EMERGENCY EXIT?
NOPE, NO ONE.
NO ONE, EH?
LISTEN, OLD MAN.
WHO YOU CALLIN' OLD MAN!? I-I'M NOT EVEN...!
COULD IT BE MR. POLICE- MAN'S DOUBTING ME?
ANY- WAY...
THAT FRIEND OF HERS IS JUST BEING OVERLY EMOTIONAL.
IN THE END, YOU'LL SETTLE FOR EITHER AN ACCIDENT OR SUICIDE, RIGHT?

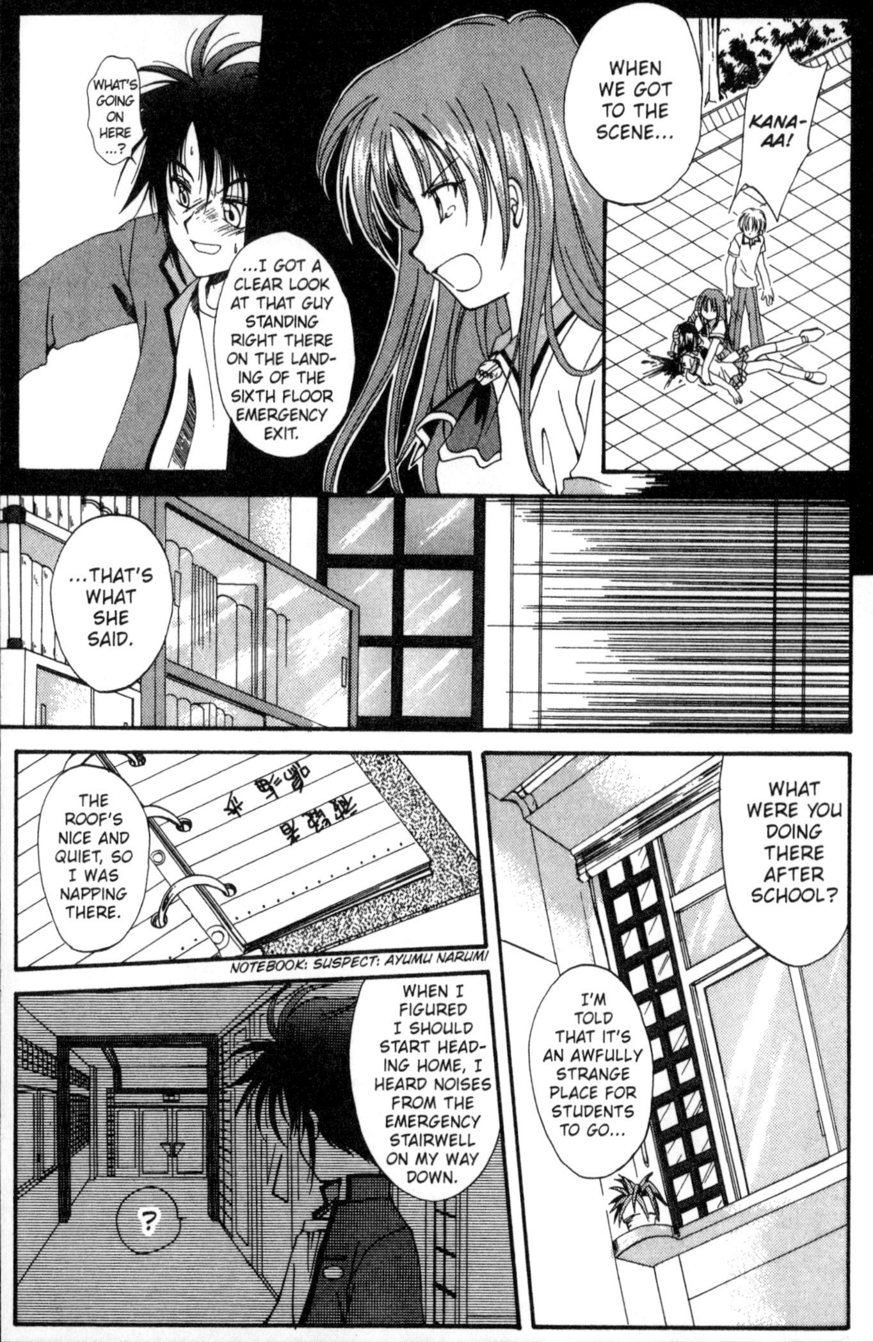
KANA-AA!
WHEN WE GOT TO THE SCENE...
...I GOT A CLEAR LOOK AT THAT GUY STANDING RIGHT THERE ON THE LANDING OF THE SIXTH FLOOR EMERGENCY EXIT.
WHAT'S GOING ON HERE ...?
...THAT'S WHAT SHE SAID.
WHAT WERE YOU DOING THERE AFTER SCHOOL?
I'M TOLD THAT IT'S AN AWFULLY STRANGE PLACE FOR STUDENTS TO GO...
THE ROOF'S NICE AND QUIET, SO I WAS NAPPING THERE.
NOTEBOOK: SUSPECT: AYUMU NARUMI
WHEN I FIGURED I SHOULD START HEADING HOME, I HEARD NOISES FROM THE EMERGENCY STAIRWELL ON MY WAY DOWN.
?

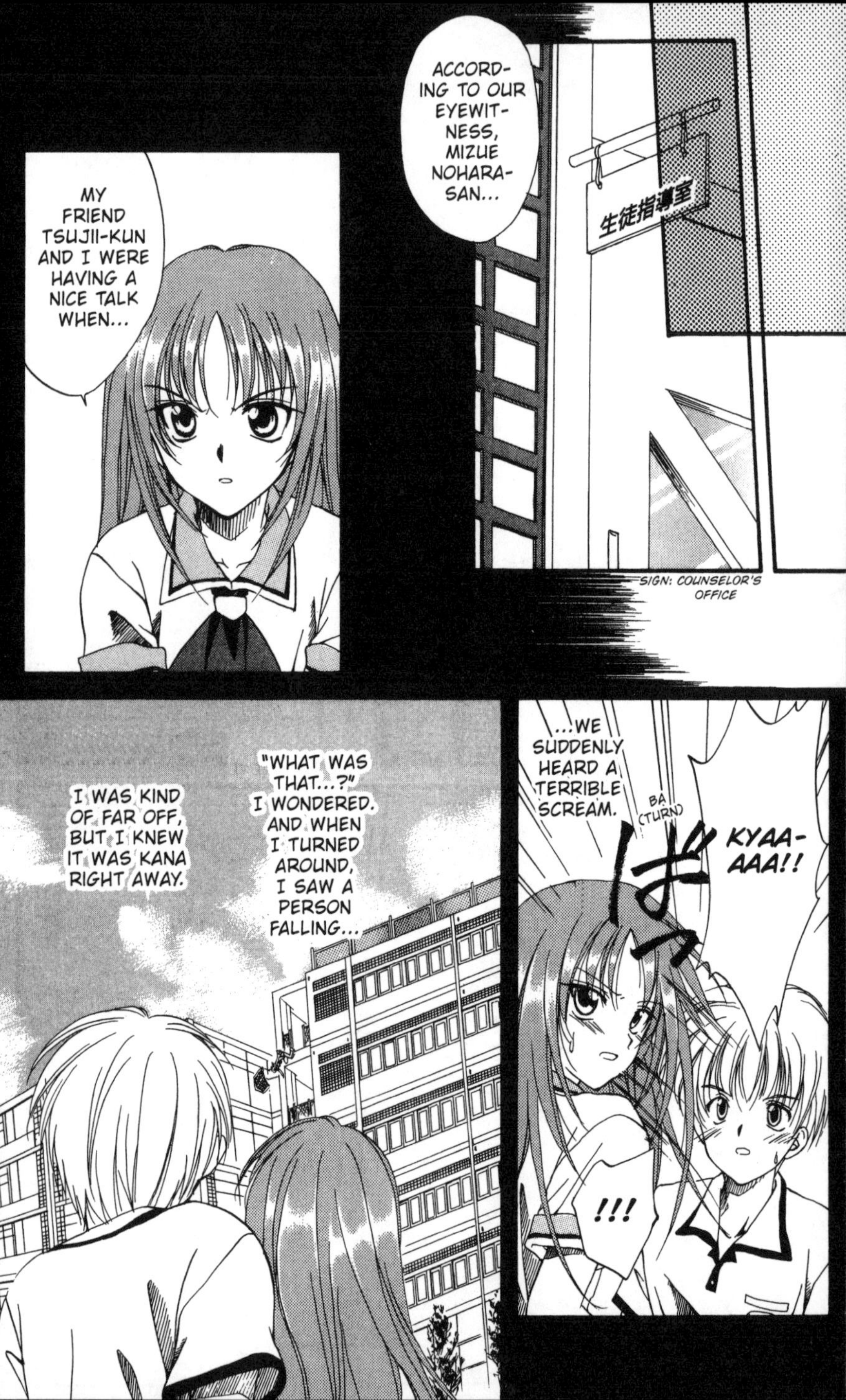

ACCORDING TO OUR EYEWITNESS, MIZUE NOHARA-SAN...
生徒指導室
SIGN: COUNSELOR'S OFFICE
MY FRIEND TSUJII-KUN AND I WERE HAVING A NICE TALK WHEN...
...WE SUDDENLY HEARD A TERRIBLE SCREAM.
KYAA-AAA!!
BA (TURN)
!!!
"WHAT WAS THAT...?" I WONDERED. AND WHEN I TURNED AROUND, I SAW A PERSON FALLING...
I WAS KIND OF FAR OFF, BUT I KNEW IT WAS KANA RIGHT AWAY.

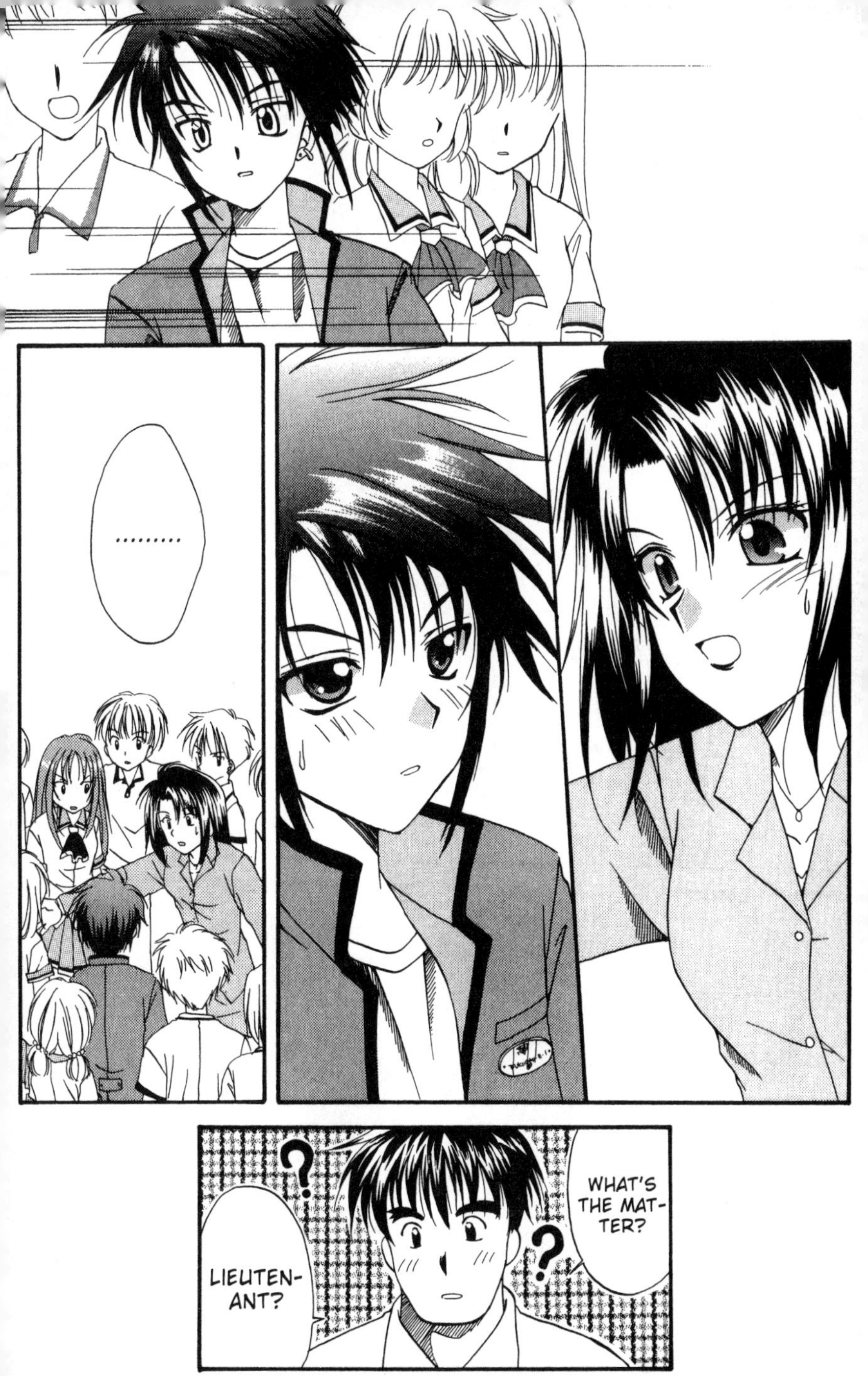
....
WHAT'S THE MAT-TER?
LIEUTEN-ANT?

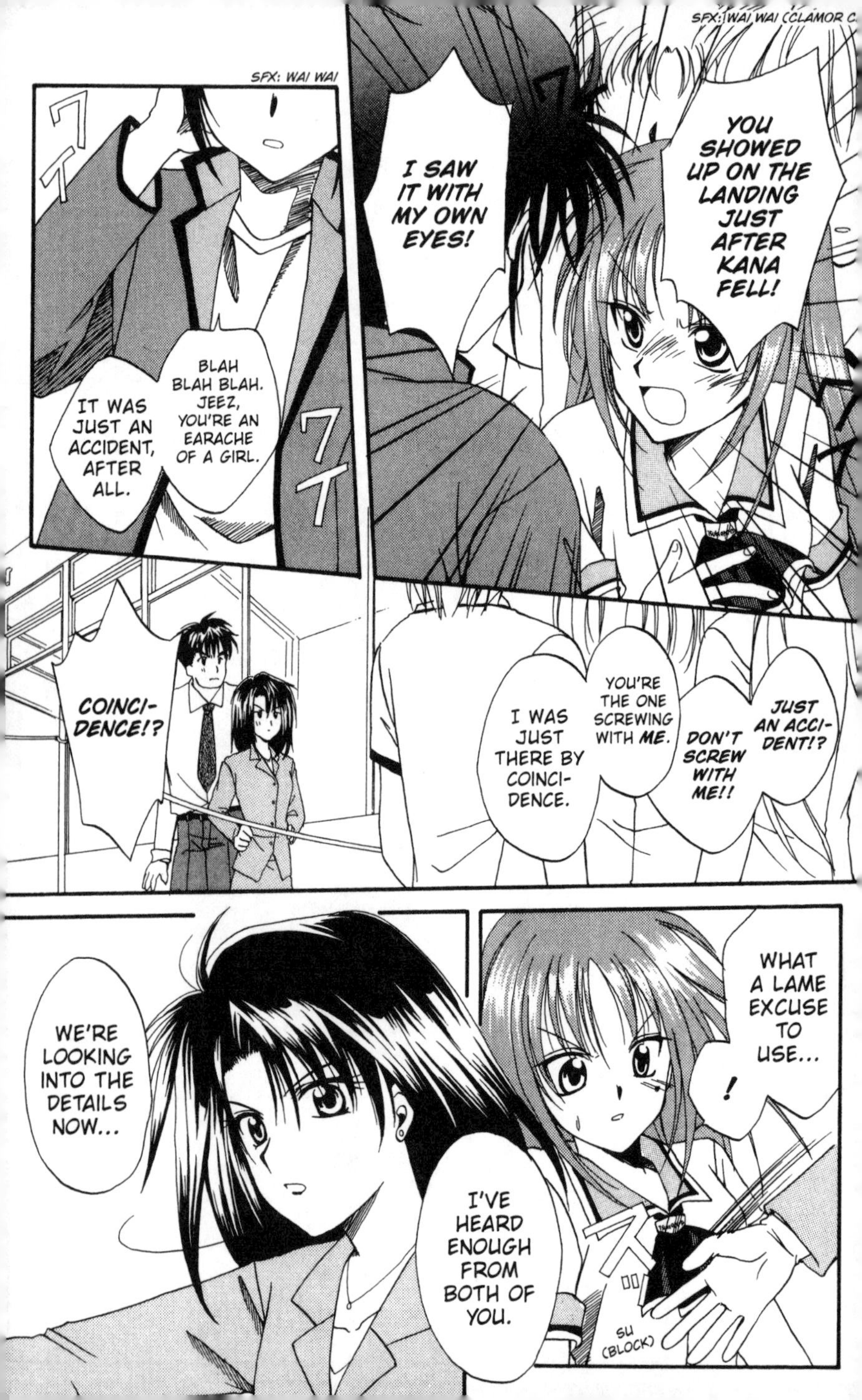
SFX: WAI WAI (CLAMOR C
YOU SHOWED UP ON THE LANDING JUST AFTER KANA FELL!
I SAW IT WITH MY OWN EYES!
SFX: WAI WAI
BLAH BLAH BLAH. JEEZ, YOU'RE AN EARACHE OF A GIRL.
IT WAS JUST AN ACCIDENT, AFTER ALL.
JUST AN ACCI-DENT!?
DON'T SCREW WITH ME!!
YOU'RE THE ONE SCREWING WITH ME.
I WAS JUST THERE BY COINCI-DENCE.
COINCI-DENCE!?
WHAT A LAME EXCUSE TO USE...
!
I'VE HEARD ENOUGH FROM BOTH OF YOU.
SU (BLOCK)
WE'RE LOOKING INTO THE DETAILS NOW...

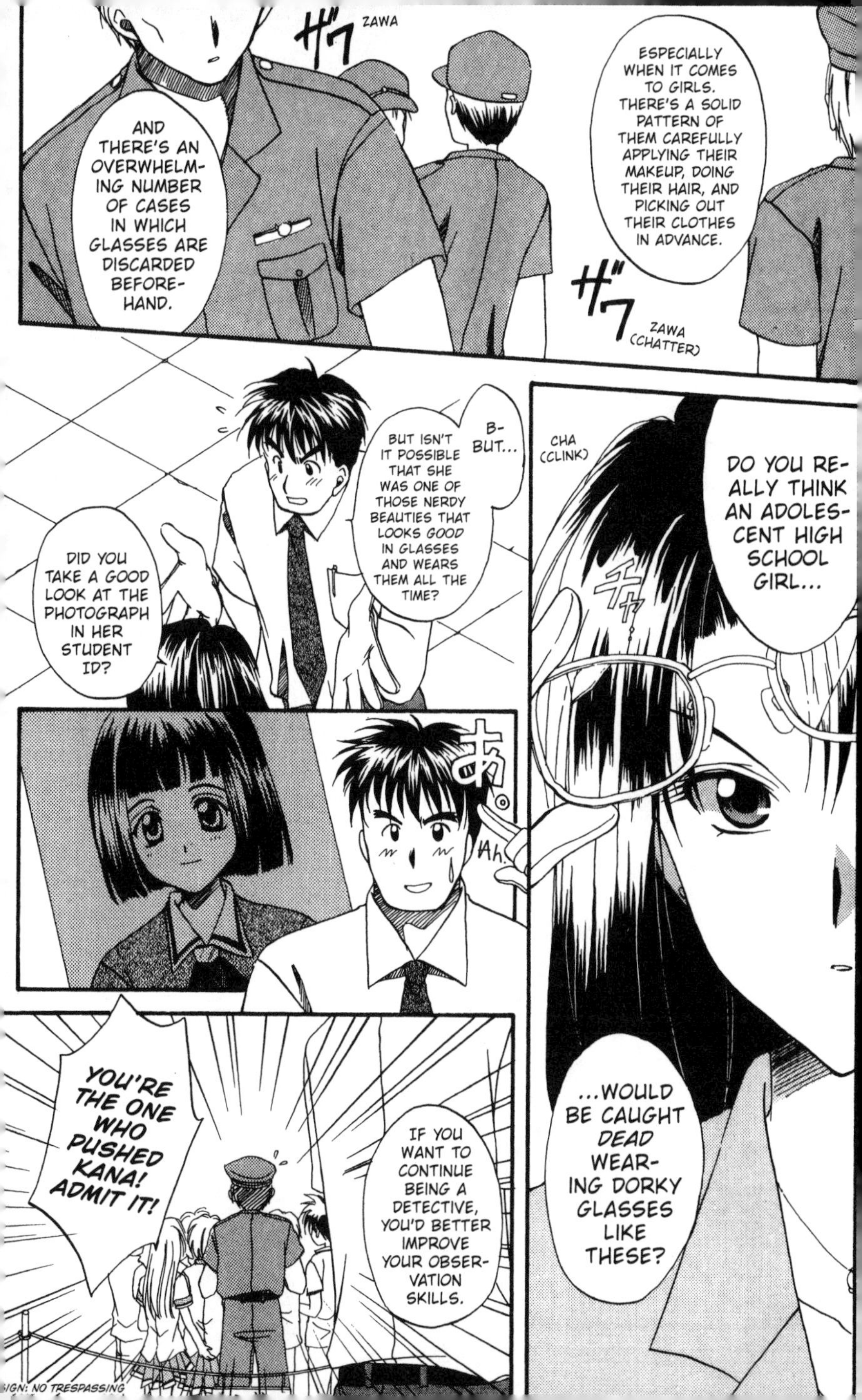
ESPECIALLY WHEN IT COMES TO GIRLS. THERE'S A SOLID PATTERN OF THEM CAREFULLY APPLYING THEIR MAKEUP, DOING THEIR HAIR, AND PICKING OUT THEIR CLOTHES IN ADVANCE.
ZAWA
AND THERE'S AN OVERWHELMING NUMBER OF CASES IN WHICH GLASSES ARE DISCARDED BEFOREHAND.
ZAWA (CHATTER)
CHA (CLINK)
DO YOU REALLY THINK AN ADOLESCENT HIGH SCHOOL GIRL...
...WOULD BE CAUGHT DEAD WEARING DORKY GLASSES LIKE THESE?
B-BUT...
BUT ISN'T IT POSSIBLE THAT SHE WAS ONE OF THOSE NERDY BEAUTIES THAT LOOKS GOOD IN GLASSES AND WEARS THEM ALL THE TIME?
DID YOU TAKE A GOOD LOOK AT THE PHOTOGRAPH IN HER STUDENT ID?
Ah.
IF YOU WANT TO CONTINUE BEING A DETECTIVE, YOU'D BETTER IMPROVE YOUR OBSERVATION SKILLS.
YOU'RE THE ONE WHO PUSHED KANA! ADMIT IT!
SIGN: NO TRESPASSING

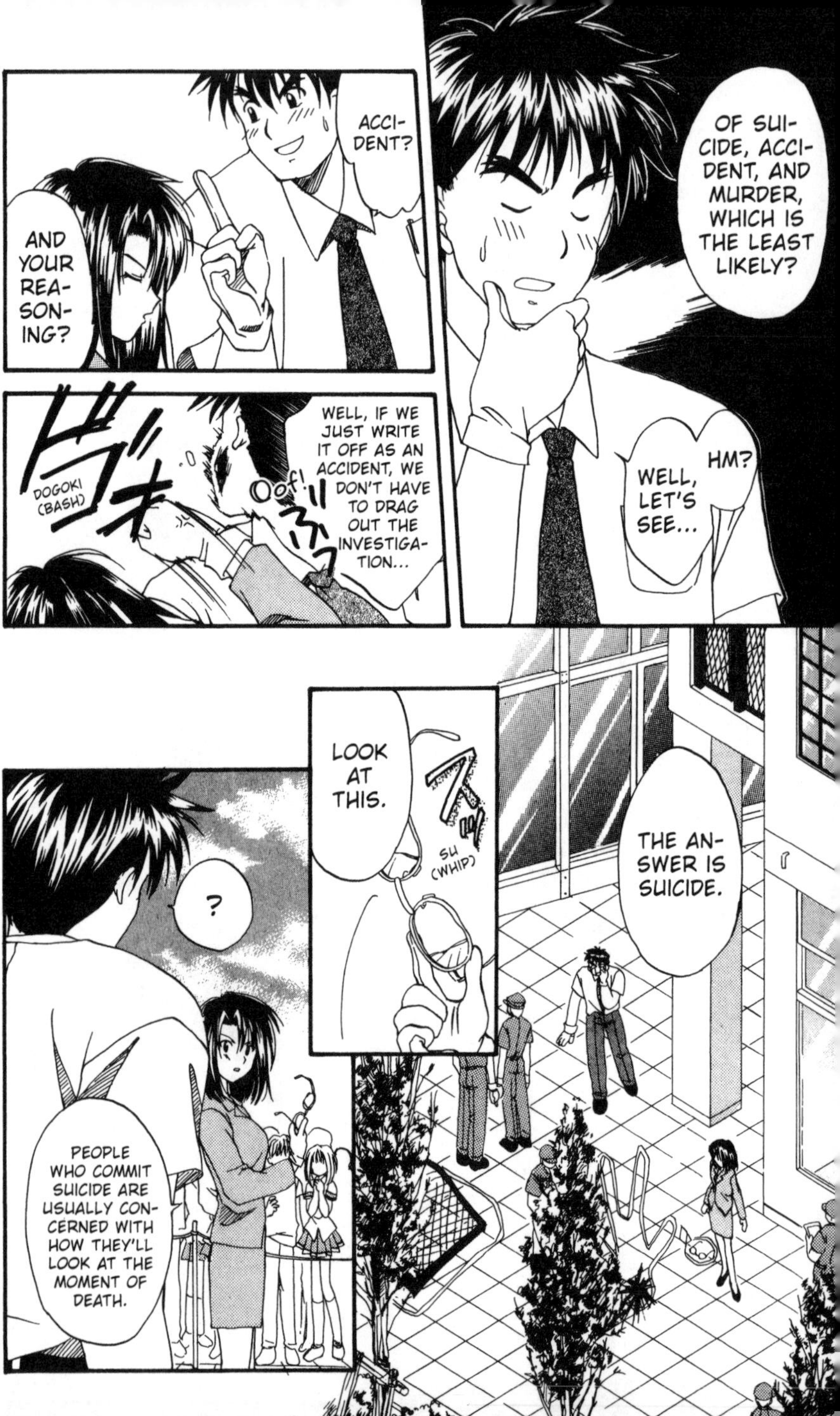
OF SUI-CIDE, ACCI-DENT, AND MURDER, WHICH IS THE LEAST LIKELY?
HM?
WELL, LET'S SEE...
ACCI-DENT?
AND YOUR REA-SON-ING?
WELL, IF WE JUST WRITE IT OFF AS AN ACCIDENT, WE DON'T HAVE TO DRAG OUT THE INVESTIGA-TION...
Oof!
DOGOKI (BASH)
THE AN-SWER IS SUICIDE.
LOOK AT THIS.
SU (WHIP)
?
PEOPLE WHO COMMIT SUICIDE ARE USUALLY CON-CERNED WITH HOW THEY'LL LOOK AT THE MOMENT OF DEATH.

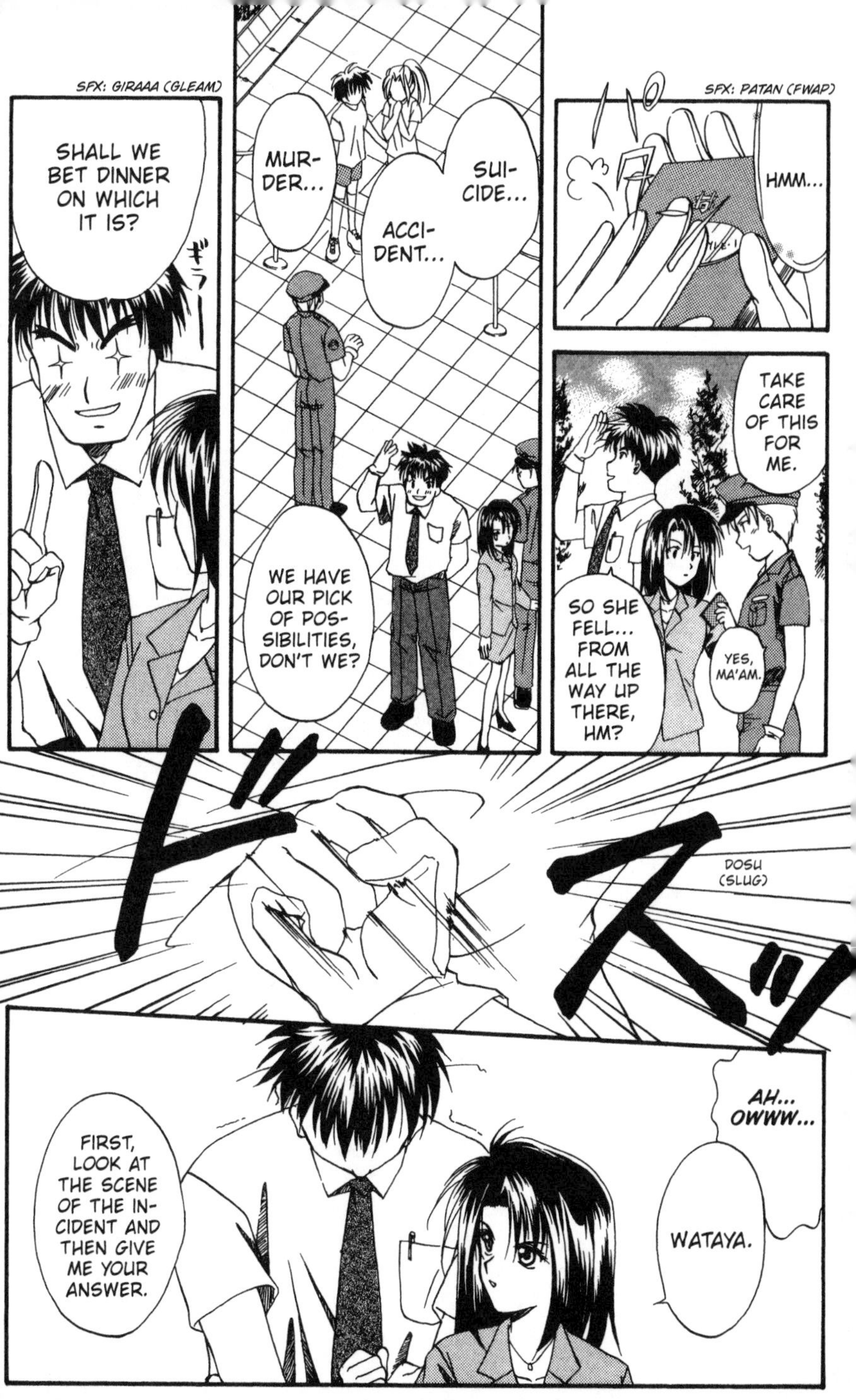
SFX: PATAN (FWAP)
HMM...
TAKE CARE OF THIS FOR ME.
SO SHE FELL... FROM ALL THE WAY UP THERE, HM?
YES, MA'AM.
SUI-CIDE...
MUR-DER...
ACCI-DENT...
WE HAVE OUR PICK OF POS-SIBILITIES, DON'T WE?
SFX: GIRAAA (GLEAM)
SHALL WE BET DINNER ON WHICH IT IS?
DOSU (SLUG)
AH... OWWW...
WATAYA.
FIRST, LOOK AT THE SCENE OF THE IN-CIDENT AND THEN GIVE ME YOUR ANSWER.

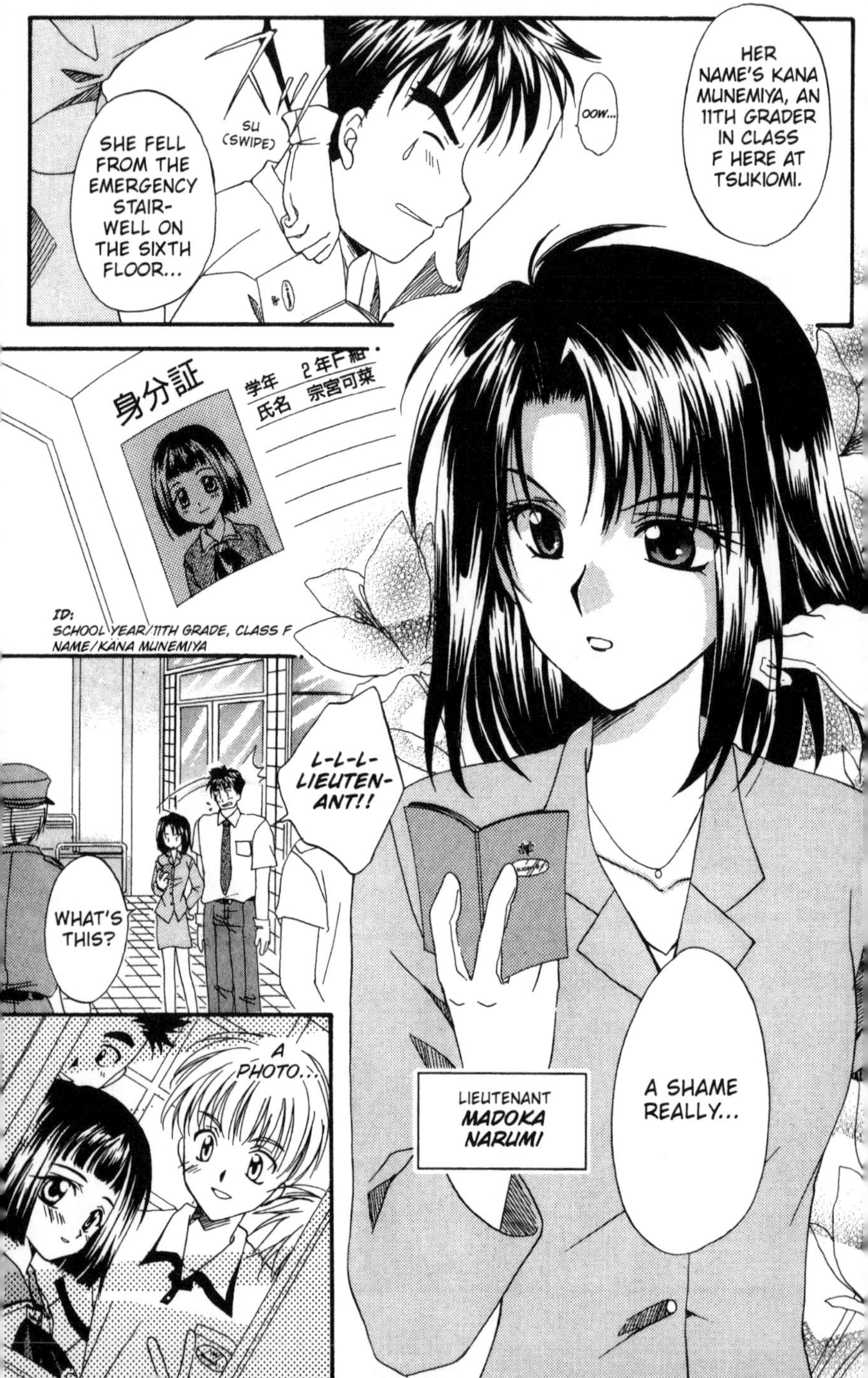
HER NAME'S KANA MUNEMIYA, AN 11TH GRADER IN CLASS F HERE AT TSUKIOMI.
OOW...
SU (SWIPE)
SHE FELL FROM THE EMERGENCY STAIR-WELL ON THE SIXTH FLOOR...
A SHAME REALLY...
LIEUTENANT MADOKA NARUMI
身分証
学年 2年F組
氏名 宗宮可菜
ID: SCHOOL YEAR/11TH GRADE, CLASS F NAME/KANA MUNEMIYA
L-L-L-LIEUTEN-ANT!!
WHAT'S THIS?
A PHOTO...

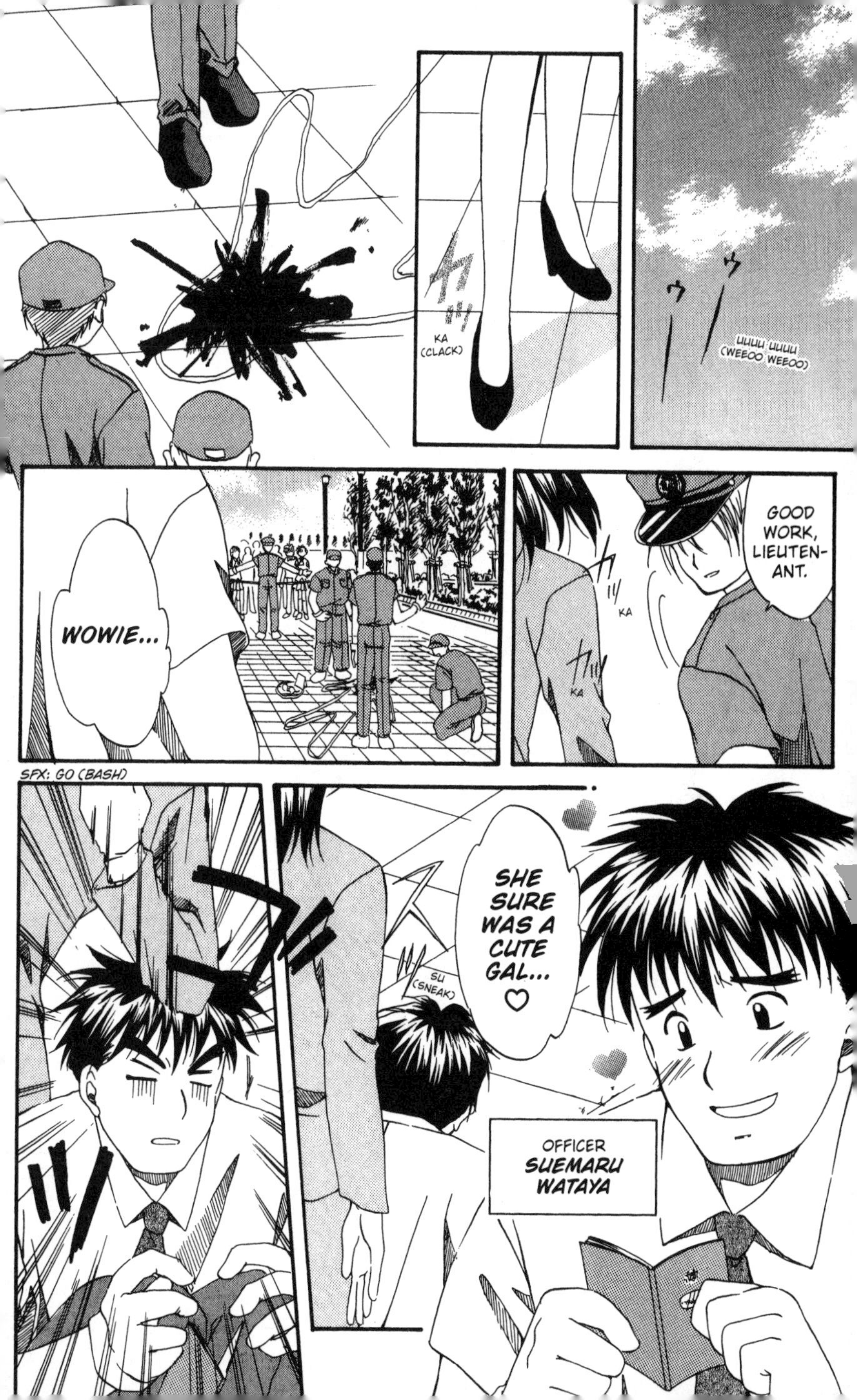
UUUU UUUU
(WEEOO WEEOO)
KA
(CLACK)
GOOD WORK, LIEUTENANT.
KA
KA
WOWIE...
SFX: GO (BASH)
SHE SURE WAS A CUTE GAL... ♡
SU
(SNEAK)
OFFICER SUEMARU WATAYA

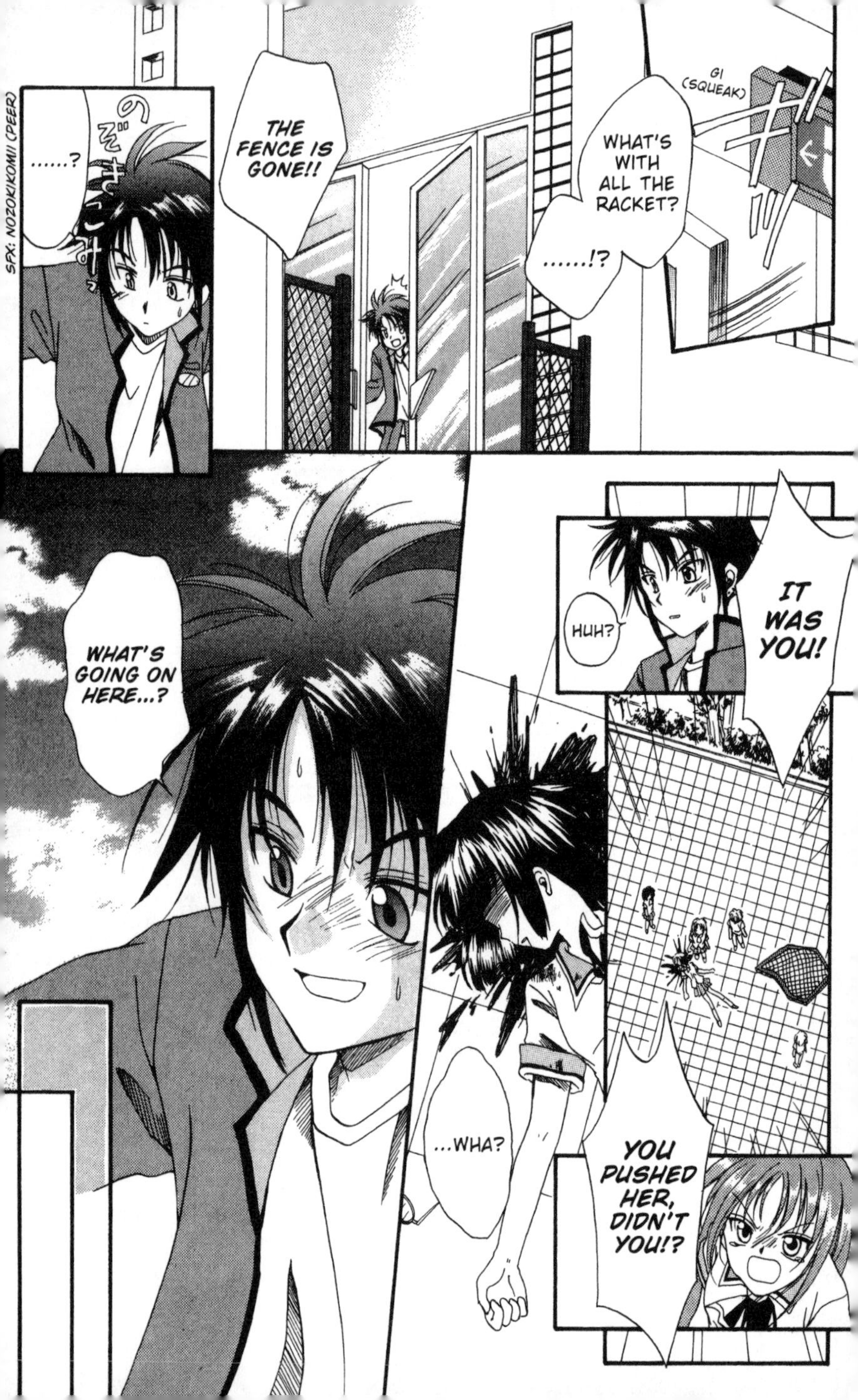
GI (SQUEAK)
WHAT'S WITH ALL THE RACKET?
......!?
THE FENCE IS GONE!!
......?
SFX: NOZOKIKOMI! (PEER)
IT WAS YOU!
HUH?
YOU PUSHED HER, DIDN'T YOU!?
...WHA?
WHAT'S GOING ON HERE...?

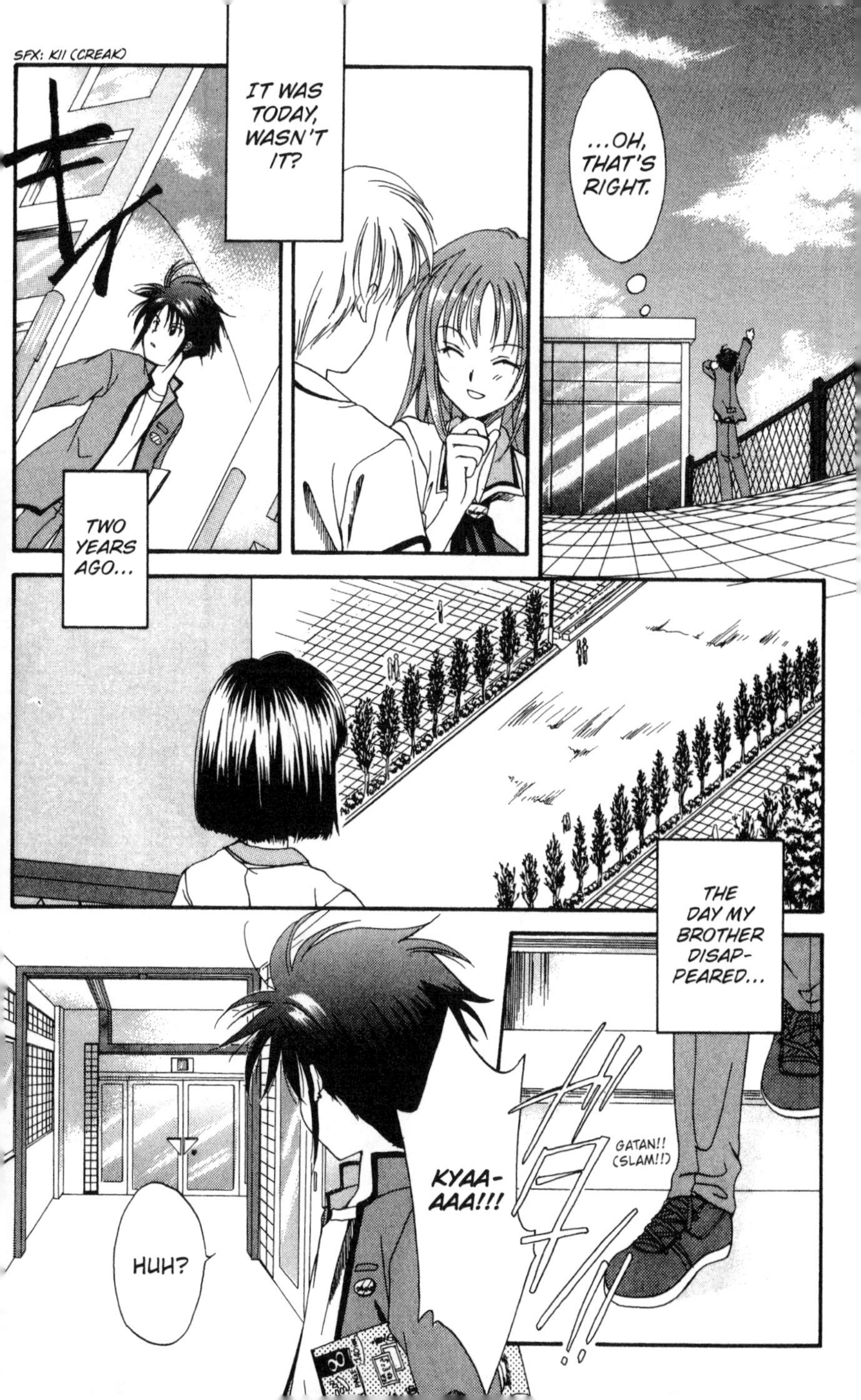
...OH, THAT'S RIGHT.
IT WAS TODAY, WASN'T IT?
SFX: KII (CREAK)
TWO YEARS AGO...
THE DAY MY BROTHER DISAPPEARED...
GATAN!! (SLAM!!)
KYAA-AAA!!!
HUH?

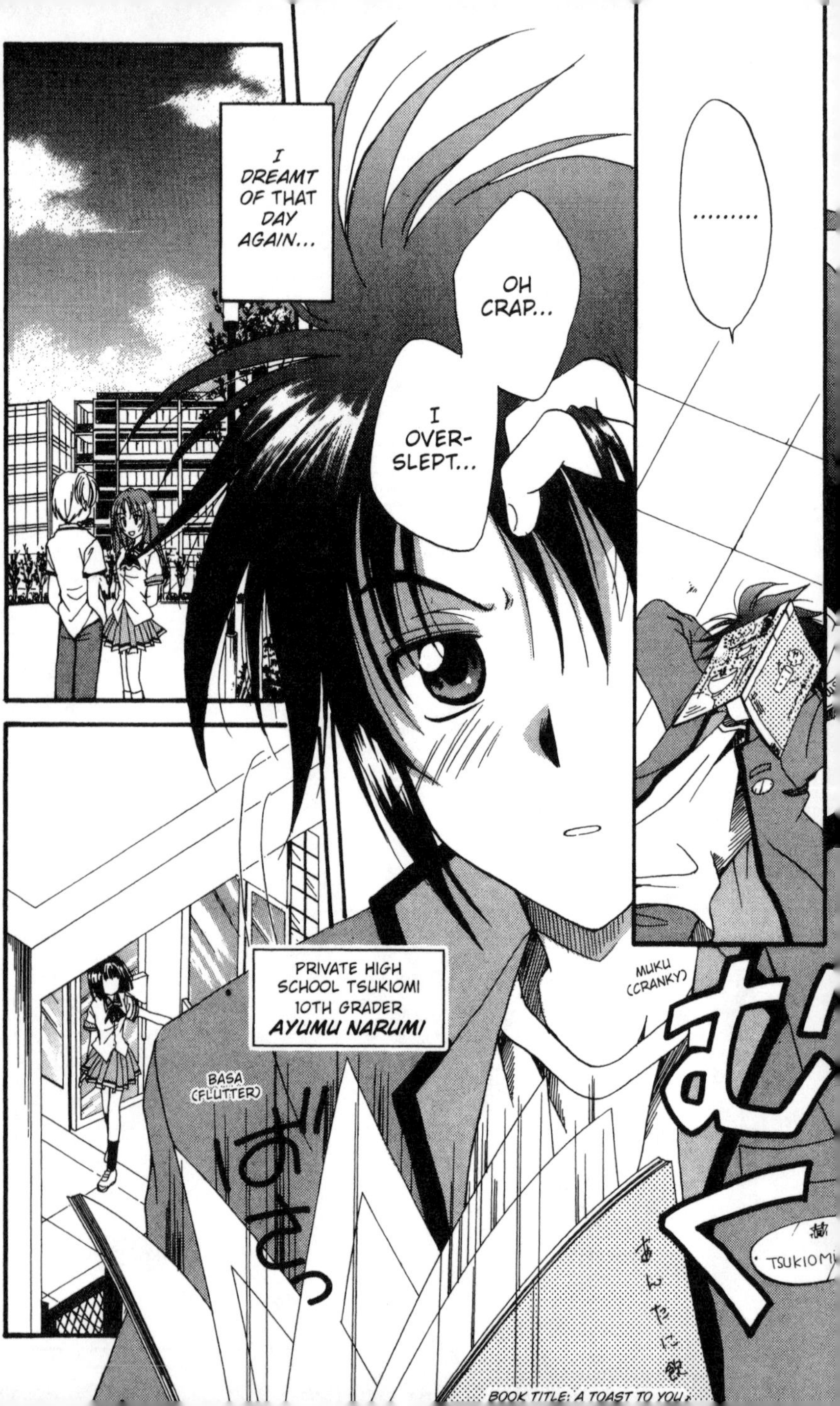
....
MUKU (CRANKY)
むく
TSUKIOMI
BOOK TITLE: A TOAST TO YOU
I DREAMT OF THAT DAY AGAIN...
OH CRAP...
I OVER-SLEPT...
PRIVATE HIGH SCHOOL TSUKIOMI 10TH GRADER
AYUMU NARUMI
BASA (FLUTTER)

Spiral

THE BONDS OF REASONING

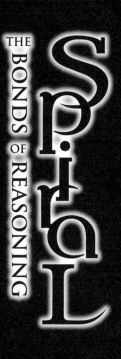

CHAPTER ONE

The Invisible Hand on the Landing (Part I)

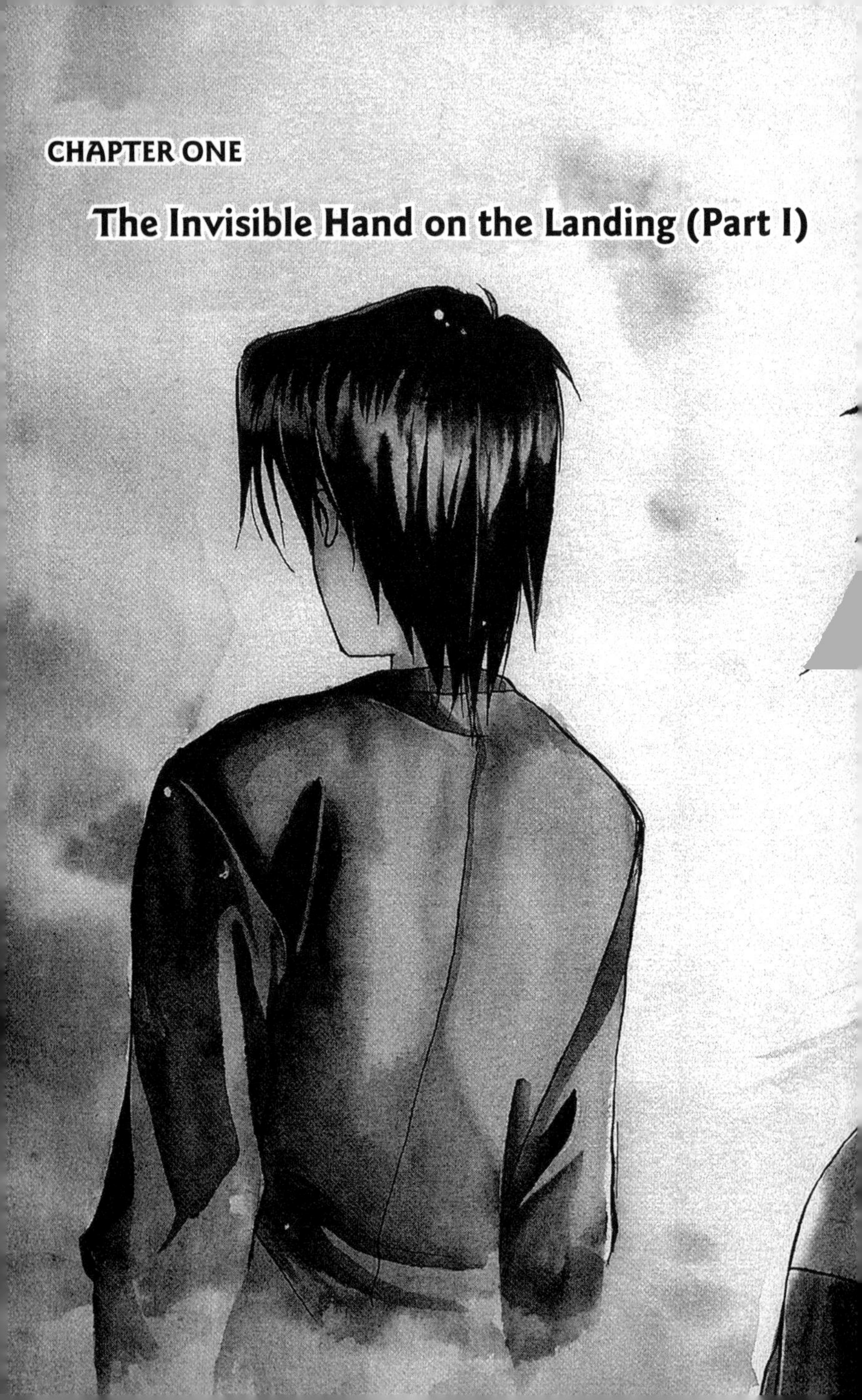

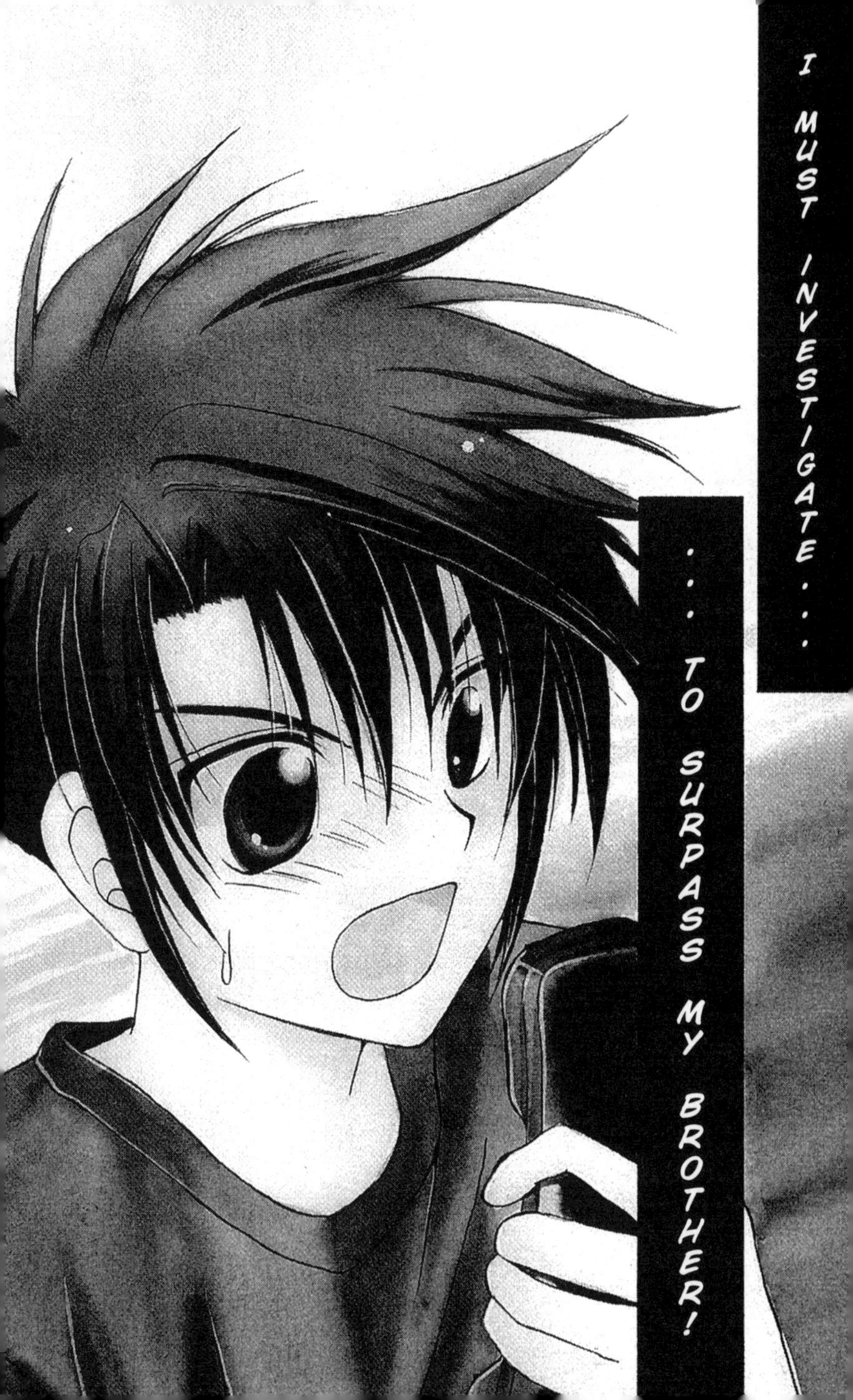
I MUST INVESTIGATE...
...TO SURPASS MY BROTHER!

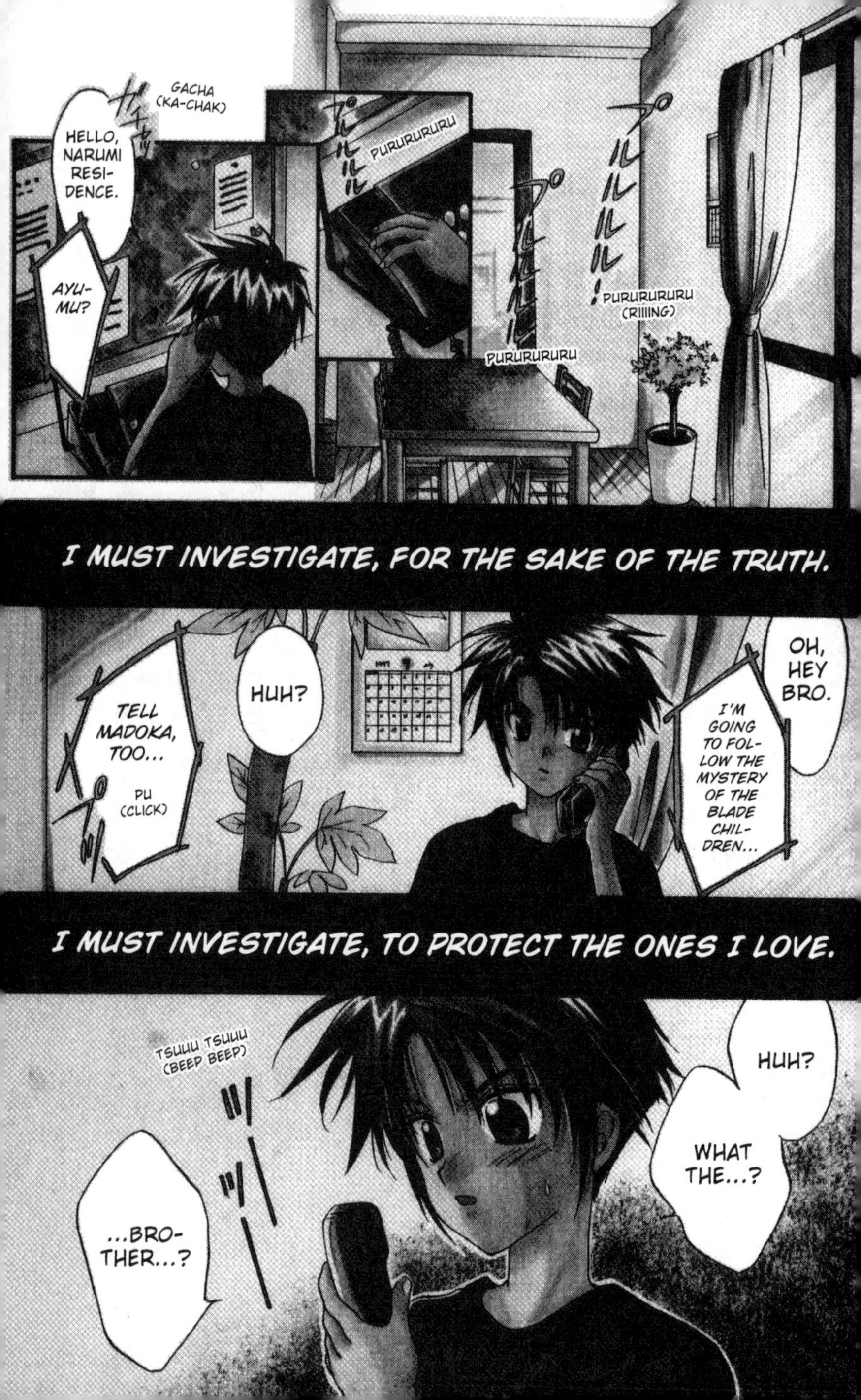
PURURURURU (RIIIING)
PURURURURU
PURURURURU
GACHA (KA-CHAK)
HELLO, NARUMI RESIDENCE.
AYUMU?
I MUST INVESTIGATE, FOR THE SAKE OF THE TRUTH.
OH, HEY BRO.
I'M GOING TO FOLLOW THE MYSTERY OF THE BLADE CHILDREN...
HUH?
TELL MADOKA, TOO...
PU (CLICK)
I MUST INVESTIGATE, TO PROTECT THE ONES I LOVE.
HUH?
WHAT THE...?
TSUUU TSUUU (BEEP BEEP)
...BROTHER...?

THE BONDS OF REASONING

Spiral

"I'm going to uncover the mystery of the 'Blade Children.'"

World-class detective Kiyotaka Narumi's last words prior to his sudden disappearance continue to haunt his younger brother, Ayumu. The cheeky 10th grader becomes further embroiled in the mystery when he is mistaken for the prime suspect in a murder at his school. Led by Ayumu's sister-in-law, Kiyotaka's wife and fellow detective, Madoka, the murder investigation gives Ayumu a chance to clear his name. But in doing so, he not only uncovers ties to the Blade Children but also more questions than answers about who and what they are.

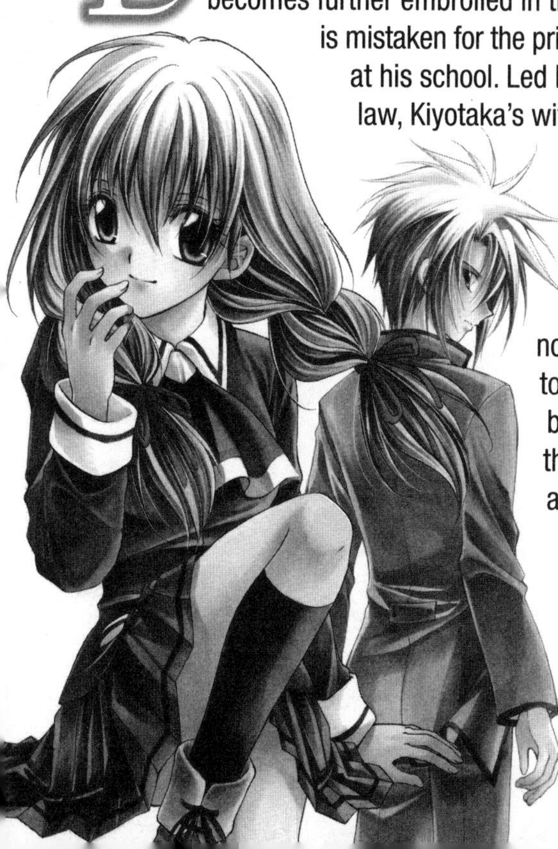

When napping on the roof leads to being accused of murder, Ayumu Narumi is left to his own devices to find the real murderer!

Spiral

THE BONDS OF REASONING

1

Story by **Kyo Shirodaira**
Art by **Eita Mizuno**

TEEN

T

L V

- ISBN-13: 978-0-7595-2341-8
- ISBN-10: 0-7595-2341-X
- $10.99 USD/$12.75 CAN/£5.99 UK
- October 2007

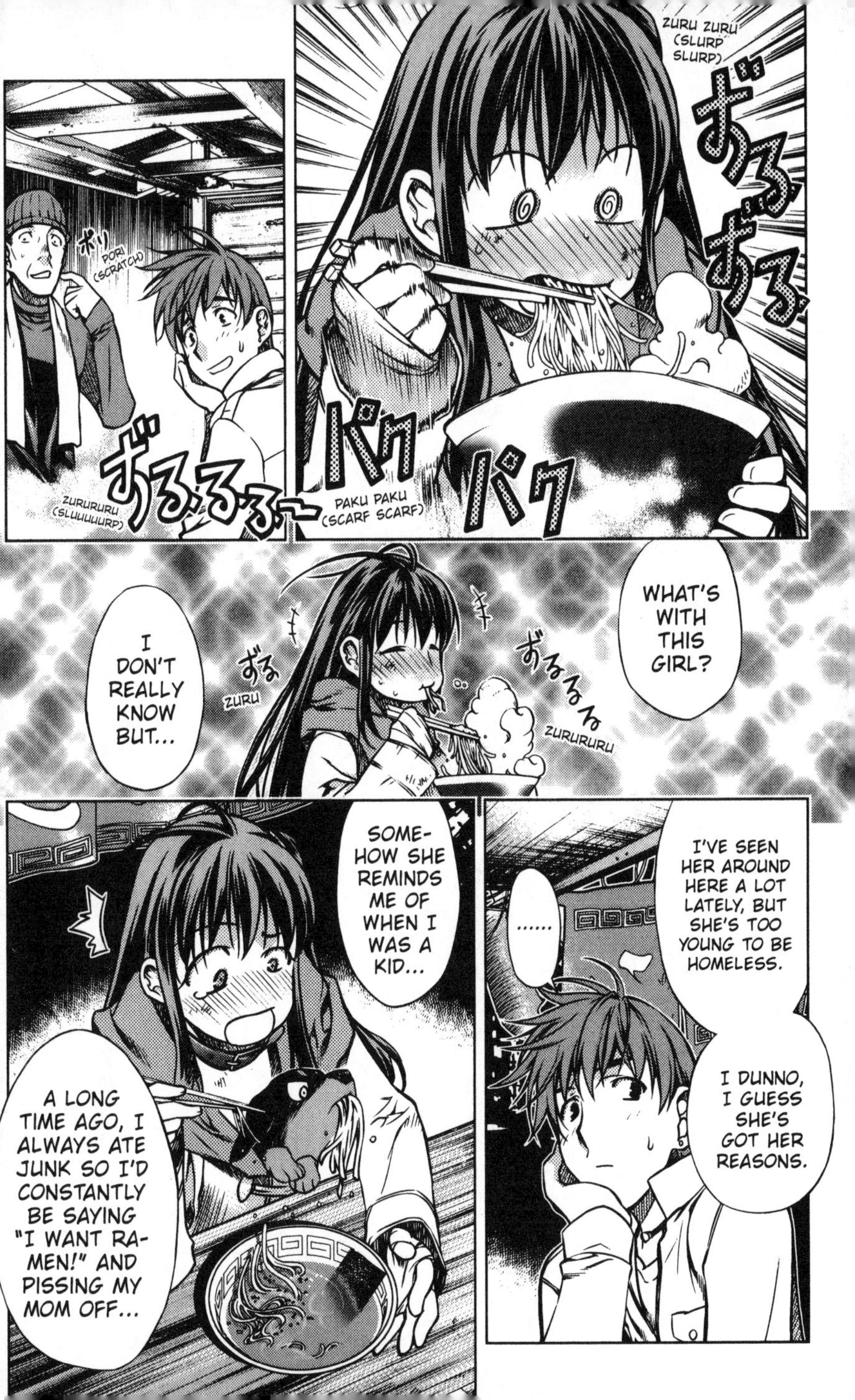
ZURU ZURU (SLURP SLURP)
ずるずる
パク パク
PAKU PAKU (SCARF SCARF)
ポリ
PORI (SCRATCH)
ずるるる~
ZURURURU (SLUUUUURP)
WHAT'S WITH THIS GIRL?
ずるるる
ZURURURU
ずる
ZURU
I DON'T REALLY KNOW BUT...
I'VE SEEN HER AROUND HERE A LOT LATELY, BUT SHE'S TOO YOUNG TO BE HOMELESS.
......
I DUNNO, I GUESS SHE'S GOT HER REASONS.
SOME-HOW SHE REMINDS ME OF WHEN I WAS A KID...
A LONG TIME AGO, I ALWAYS ATE JUNK SO I'D CONSTANTLY BE SAYING "I WANT RA-MEN!" AND PISSING MY MOM OFF...

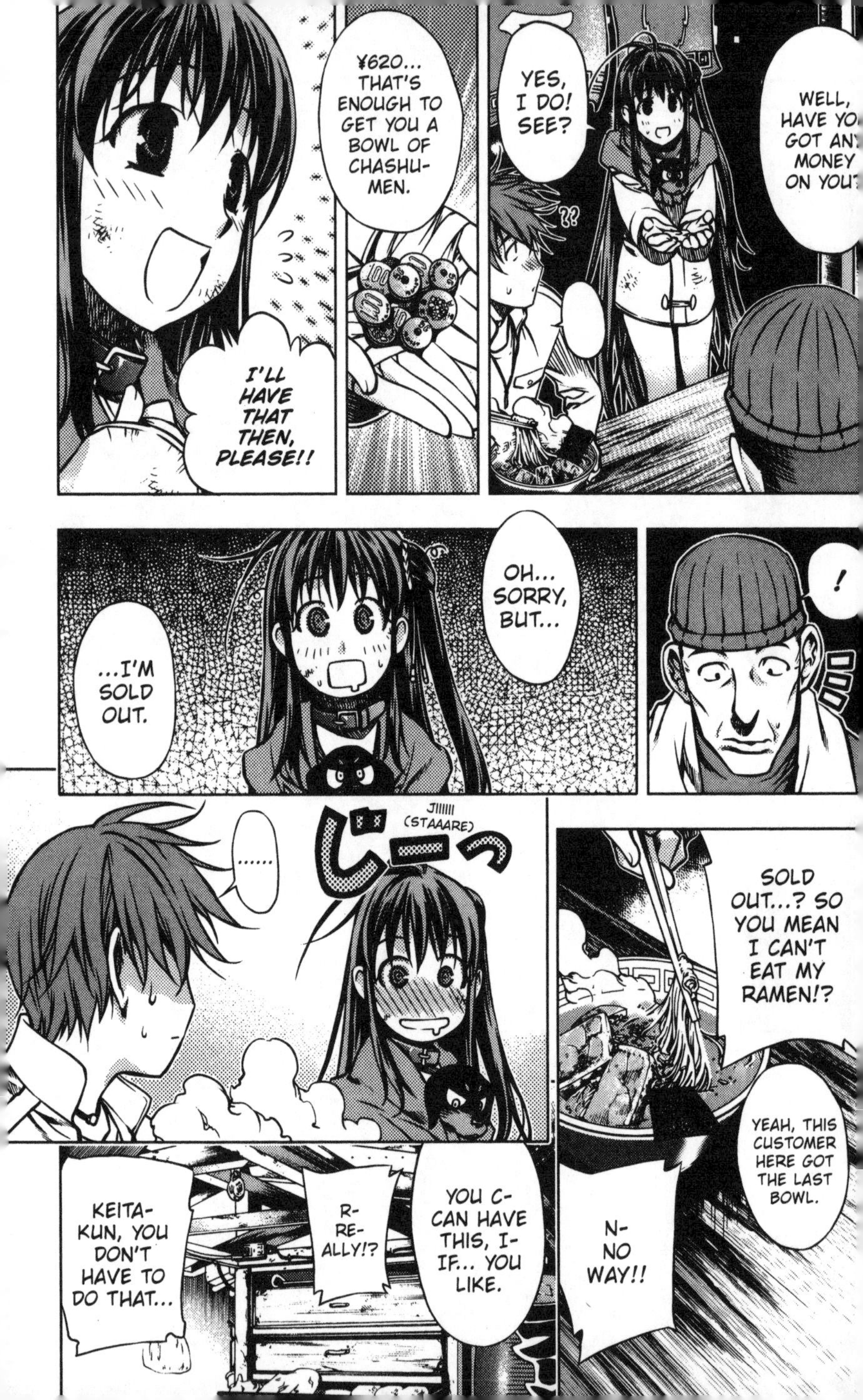

WELL, HAVE YO GOT AN MONEY ON YOU
YES, I DO! SEE?
??
¥620... THAT'S ENOUGH TO GET YOU A BOWL OF CHASHU-MEN.
I'LL HAVE THAT THEN, PLEASE!!
!
OH... SORRY, BUT...
...I'M SOLD OUT.
SOLD OUT...? SO YOU MEAN I CAN'T EAT MY RAMEN!?
YEAH, THIS CUSTOMER HERE GOT THE LAST BOWL.
N-NO WAY!!
JIIIII (STAAARE)
......
YOU C-CAN HAVE THIS, I-IF... YOU LIKE.
R-RE-ALLY!?
KEITA-KUN, YOU DON'T HAVE TO DO THAT...

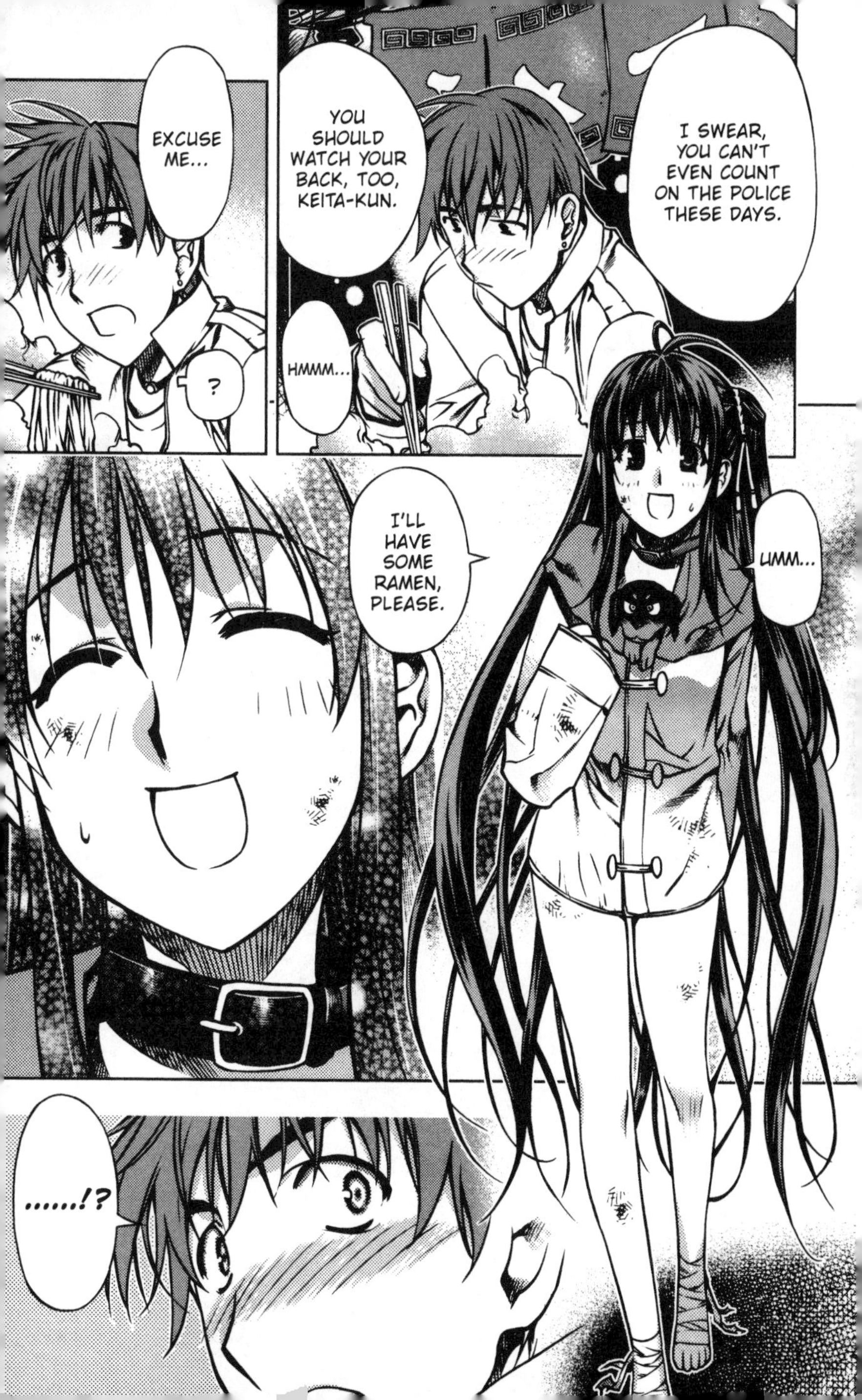
I SWEAR, YOU CAN'T EVEN COUNT ON THE POLICE THESE DAYS.
YOU SHOULD WATCH YOUR BACK, TOO, KEITA-KUN.
HMMM...
EXCUSE ME...
?
UMM...
I'LL HAVE SOME RAMEN, PLEASE.
......!?

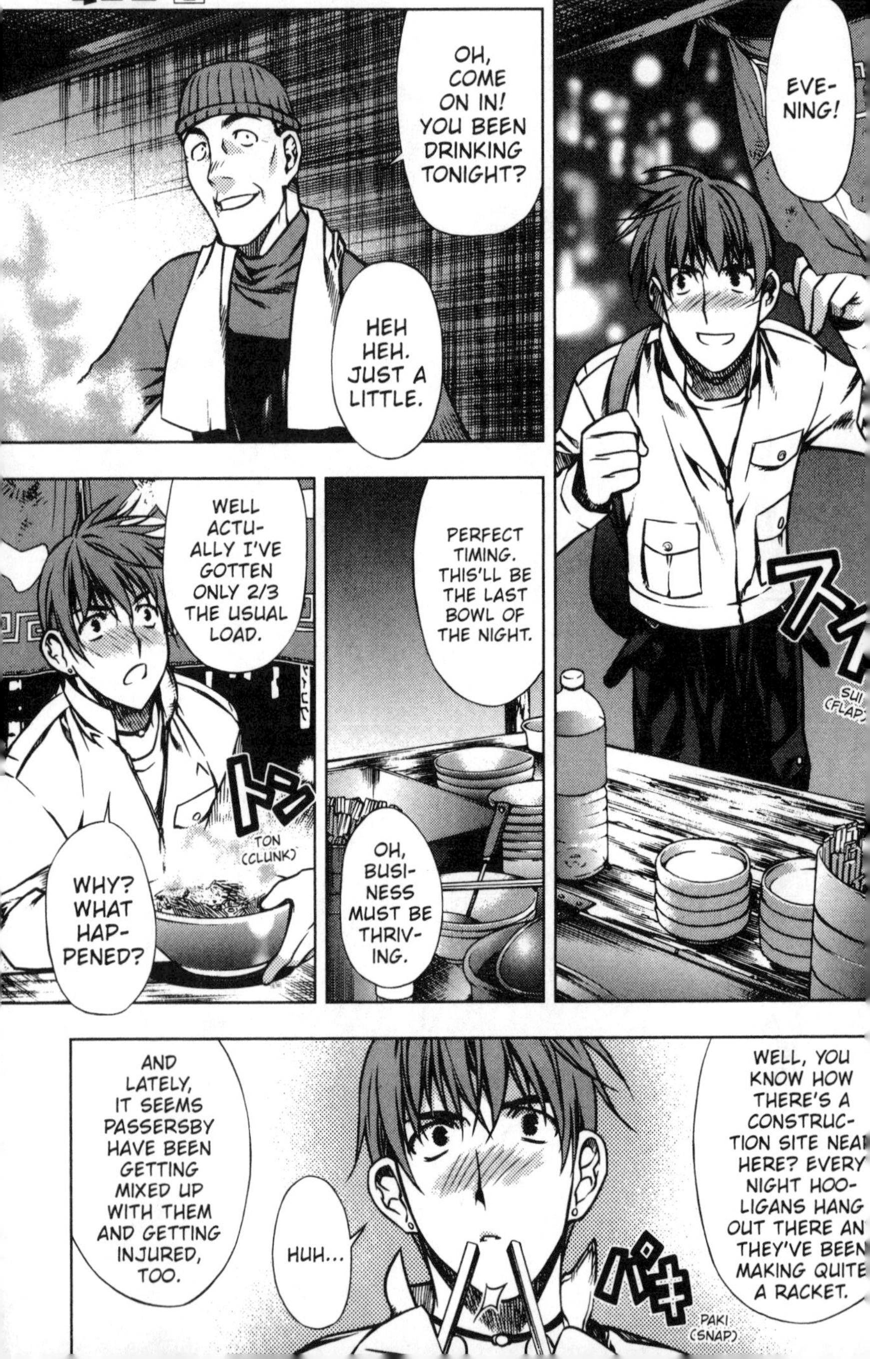
EVE-NING!
スイ
SUI (FLAP)
OH, COME ON IN! YOU BEEN DRINKING TONIGHT?
HEH HEH. JUST A LITTLE.
PERFECT TIMING. THIS'LL BE THE LAST BOWL OF THE NIGHT.
OH, BUSI-NESS MUST BE THRIV-ING.
WELL ACTU-ALLY I'VE GOTTEN ONLY 2/3 THE USUAL LOAD.
トン
TON (CLUNK)
WHY? WHAT HAP-PENED?
WELL, YOU KNOW HOW THERE'S A CONSTRUC-TION SITE NEAR HERE? EVERY NIGHT HOO-LIGANS HANG OUT THERE AND THEY'VE BEEN MAKING QUITE A RACKET.
パキ
PAKI (SNAP)
HUH...
AND LATELY, IT SEEMS PASSERSBY HAVE BEEN GETTING MIXED UP WITH THEM AND GETTING INJURED, TOO.

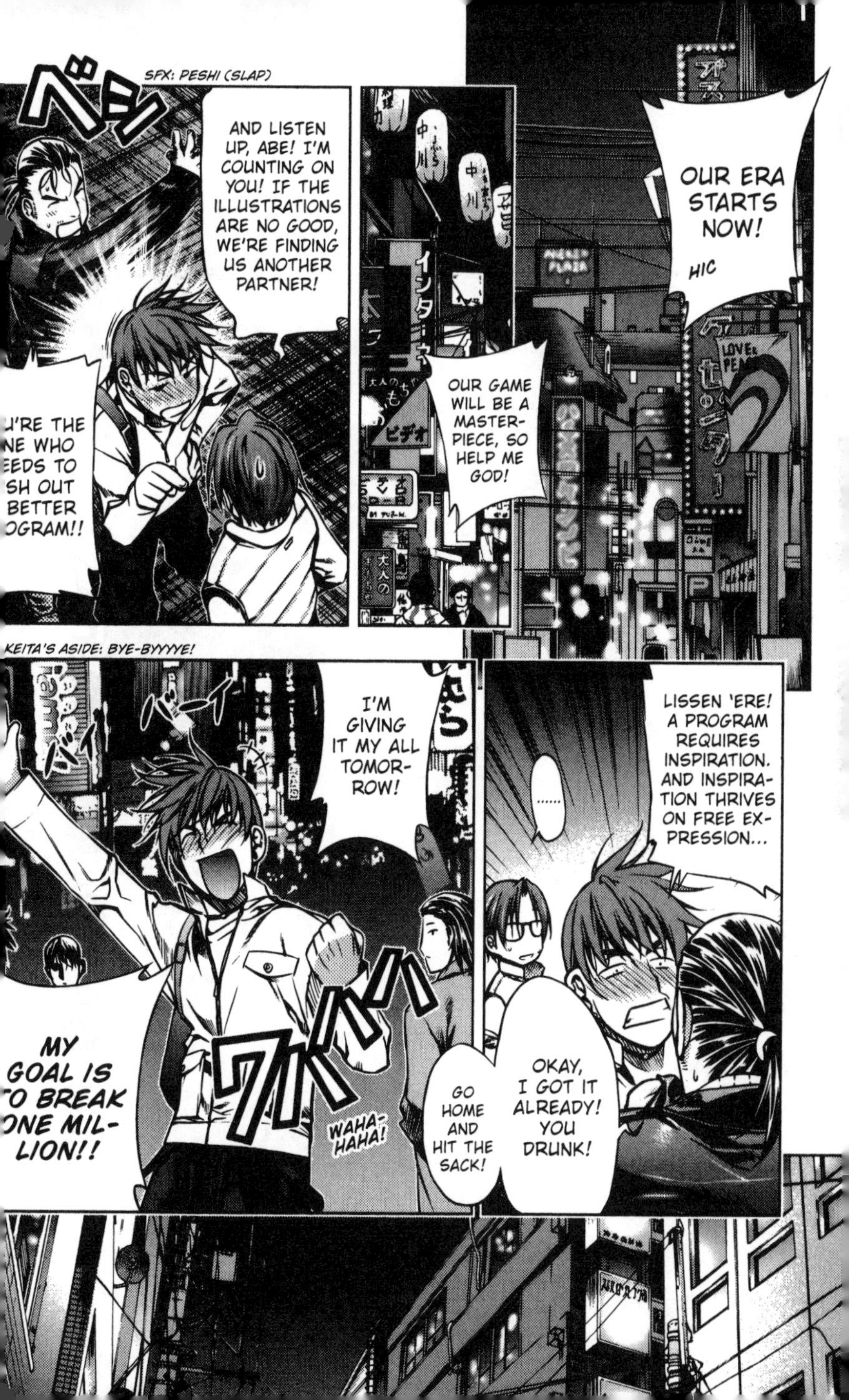
OUR ERA STARTS NOW!
HIC
OUR GAME WILL BE A MASTERPIECE, SO HELP ME GOD!
SFX: PESHI (SLAP)
AND LISTEN UP, ABE! I'M COUNTING ON YOU! IF THE ILLUSTRATIONS ARE NO GOOD, WE'RE FINDING US ANOTHER PARTNER!
U'RE THE NE WHO EEDS TO SH OUT BETTER OGRAM!!
KEITA'S ASIDE: BYE-BYYYYE!
LISSEN 'ERE! A PROGRAM REQUIRES INSPIRATION. AND INSPIRATION THRIVES ON FREE EXPRESSION...
......
OKAY, I GOT IT ALREADY! YOU DRUNK!
GO HOME AND HIT THE SACK!
I'M GIVING IT MY ALL TOMORROW!
WAHAHA!
MY GOAL IS O BREAK ONE MILLION!!

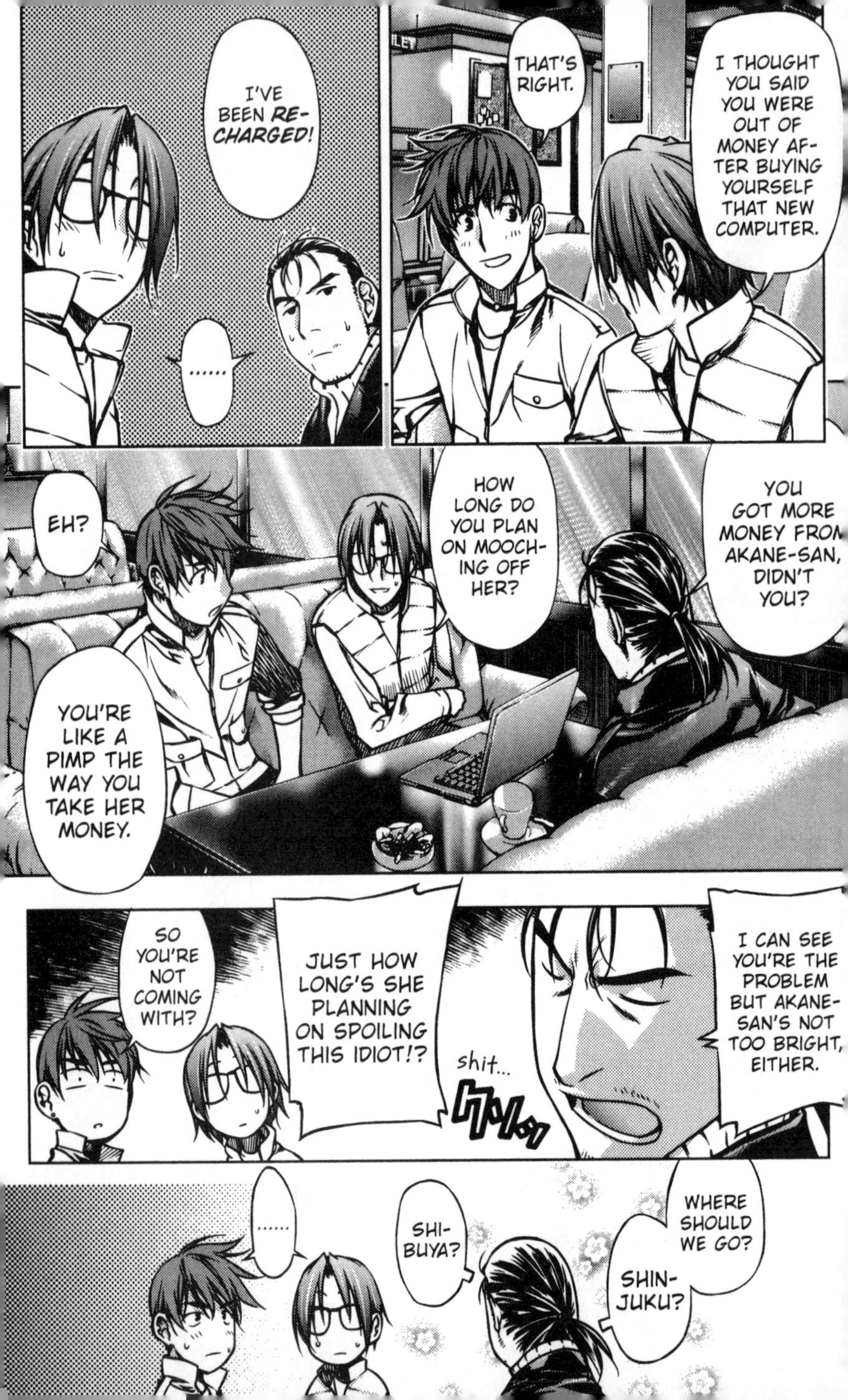
I THOUGHT YOU SAID YOU WERE OUT OF MONEY AFTER BUYING YOURSELF THAT NEW COMPUTER.
THAT'S RIGHT.
I'VE BEEN *RE-CHARGED!*
....
YOU GOT MORE MONEY FROM AKANE-SAN, DIDN'T YOU?
HOW LONG DO YOU PLAN ON MOOCHING OFF HER?
EH?
YOU'RE LIKE A PIMP THE WAY YOU TAKE HER MONEY.
I CAN SEE YOU'RE THE PROBLEM BUT AKANE-SAN'S NOT TOO BRIGHT, EITHER.
shit...
JUST HOW LONG'S SHE PLANNING ON SPOILING THIS IDIOT!?
SO YOU'RE NOT COMING WITH?
WHERE SHOULD WE GO?
SHINJUKU?
SHIBUYA?
......

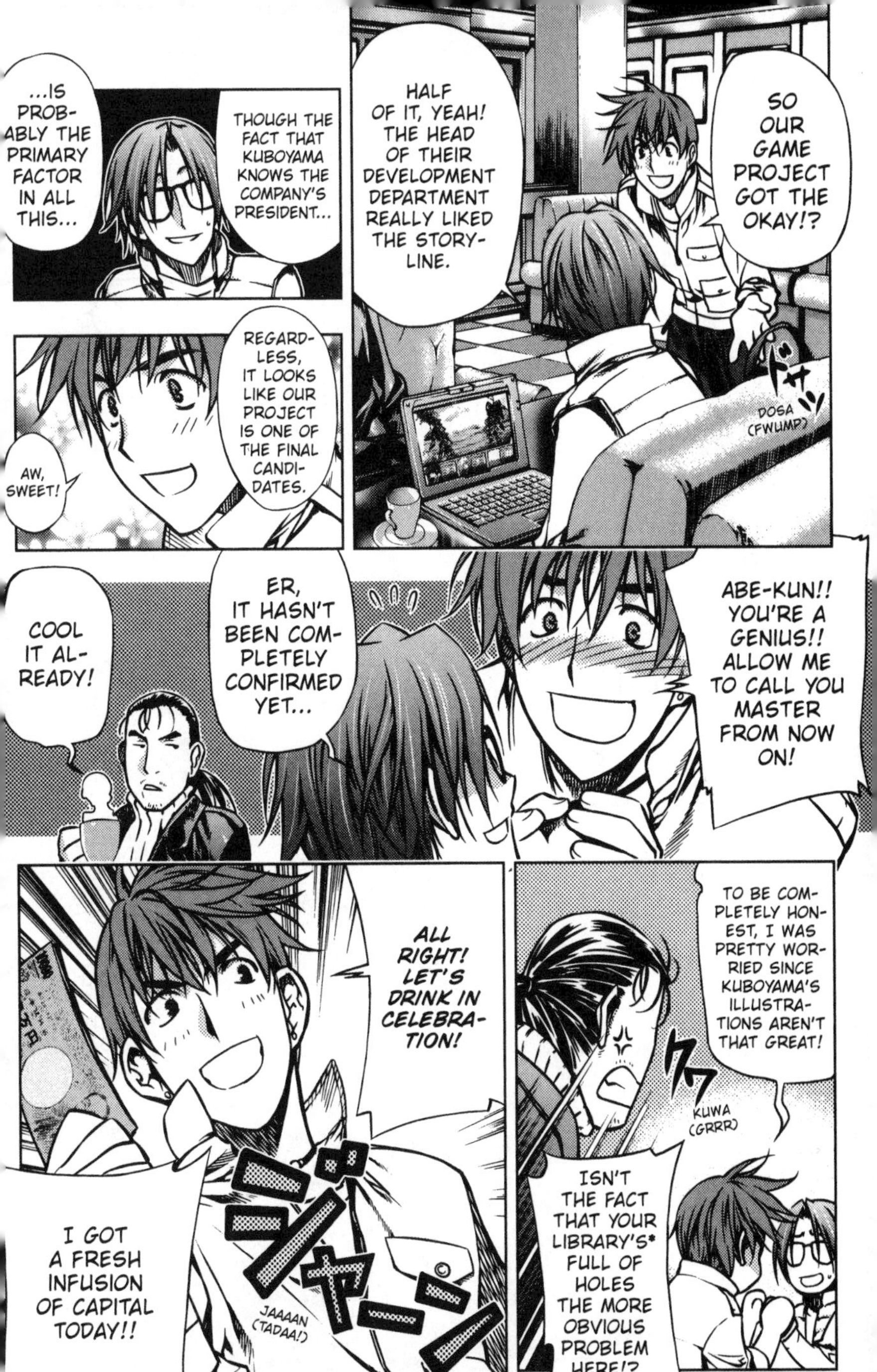
SO OUR GAME PROJECT GOT THE OKAY!?
HALF OF IT, YEAH! THE HEAD OF THEIR DEVELOPMENT DEPARTMENT REALLY LIKED THE STORY-LINE.
DOSA (FWUMP)
THOUGH THE FACT THAT KUBOYAMA KNOWS THE COMPANY'S PRESIDENT...
...IS PROB-ABLY THE PRIMARY FACTOR IN ALL THIS...
REGARD-LESS, IT LOOKS LIKE OUR PROJECT IS ONE OF THE FINAL CANDI-DATES.
AW, SWEET!
ABE-KUN!! YOU'RE A GENIUS!! ALLOW ME TO CALL YOU MASTER FROM NOW ON!
ER, IT HASN'T BEEN COM-PLETELY CONFIRMED YET...
COOL IT AL-READY!
TO BE COM-PLETELY HON-EST, I WAS PRETTY WOR-RIED SINCE KUBOYAMA'S ILLUSTRA-TIONS AREN'T THAT GREAT!
KUWA (GRRR)
ISN'T THE FACT THAT YOUR LIBRARY'S* FULL OF HOLES THE MORE OBVIOUS PROBLEM HERE!?
ALL RIGHT! LET'S DRINK IN CELEBRA-TION!
I GOT A FRESH INFUSION OF CAPITAL TODAY!!
JAAAAN (TADAA!)

* A FILE AND DATABASE AREA THAT GATHERS AND SAVES MULTIPLE DATA ITEMS AND PROGRAMS IN A COMPUTER.

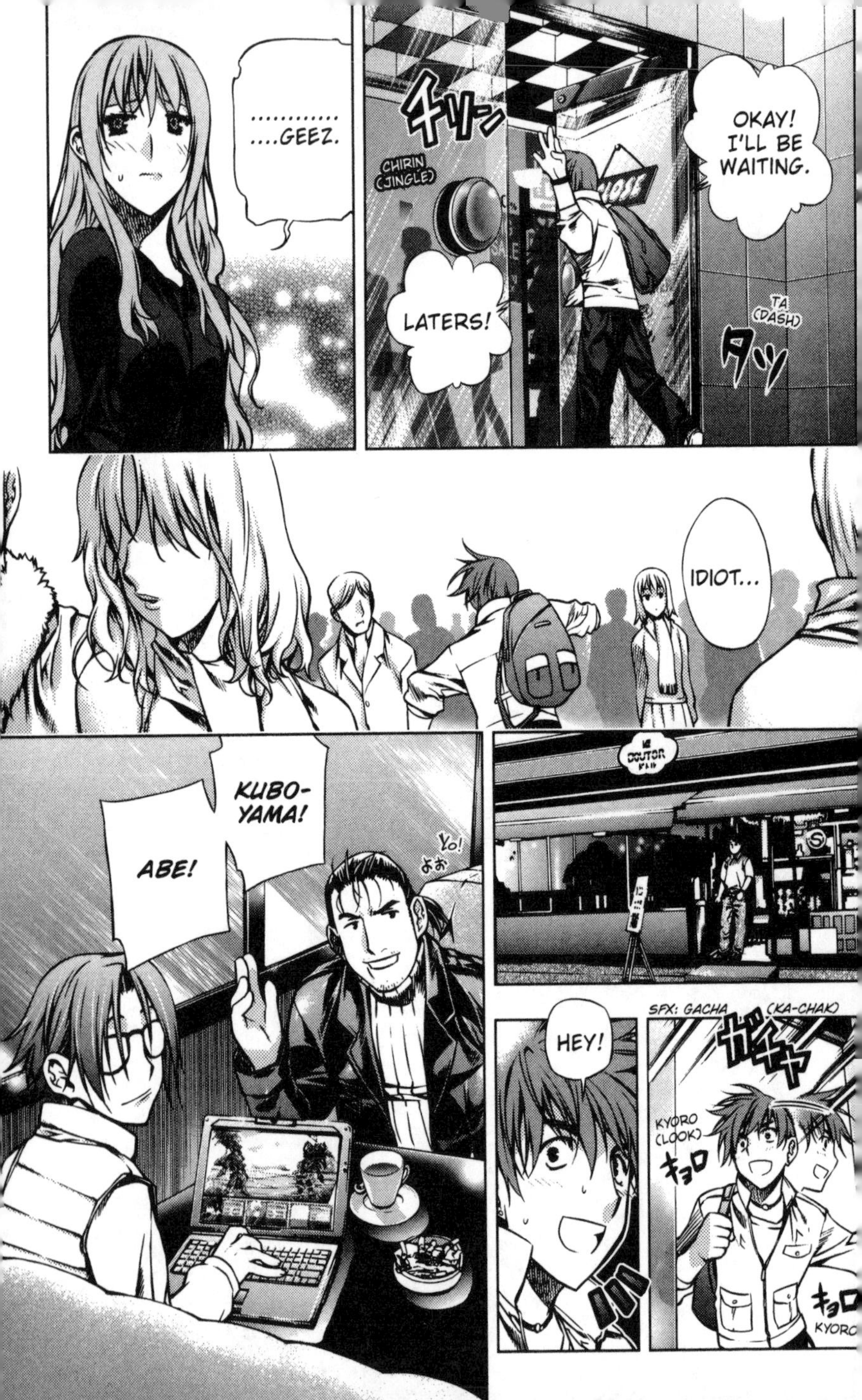
OKAY! I'LL BE WAITING.
TA (DASH)
CHIRIN (JINGLE)
LATERS!
....
....GEEZ.
IDIOT...
DOUTOR
SFX: GACHA (KA-CHAK)
KYORO (LOOK)
KYORO
HEY!
KUBO-YAMA!
ABE!
YO!

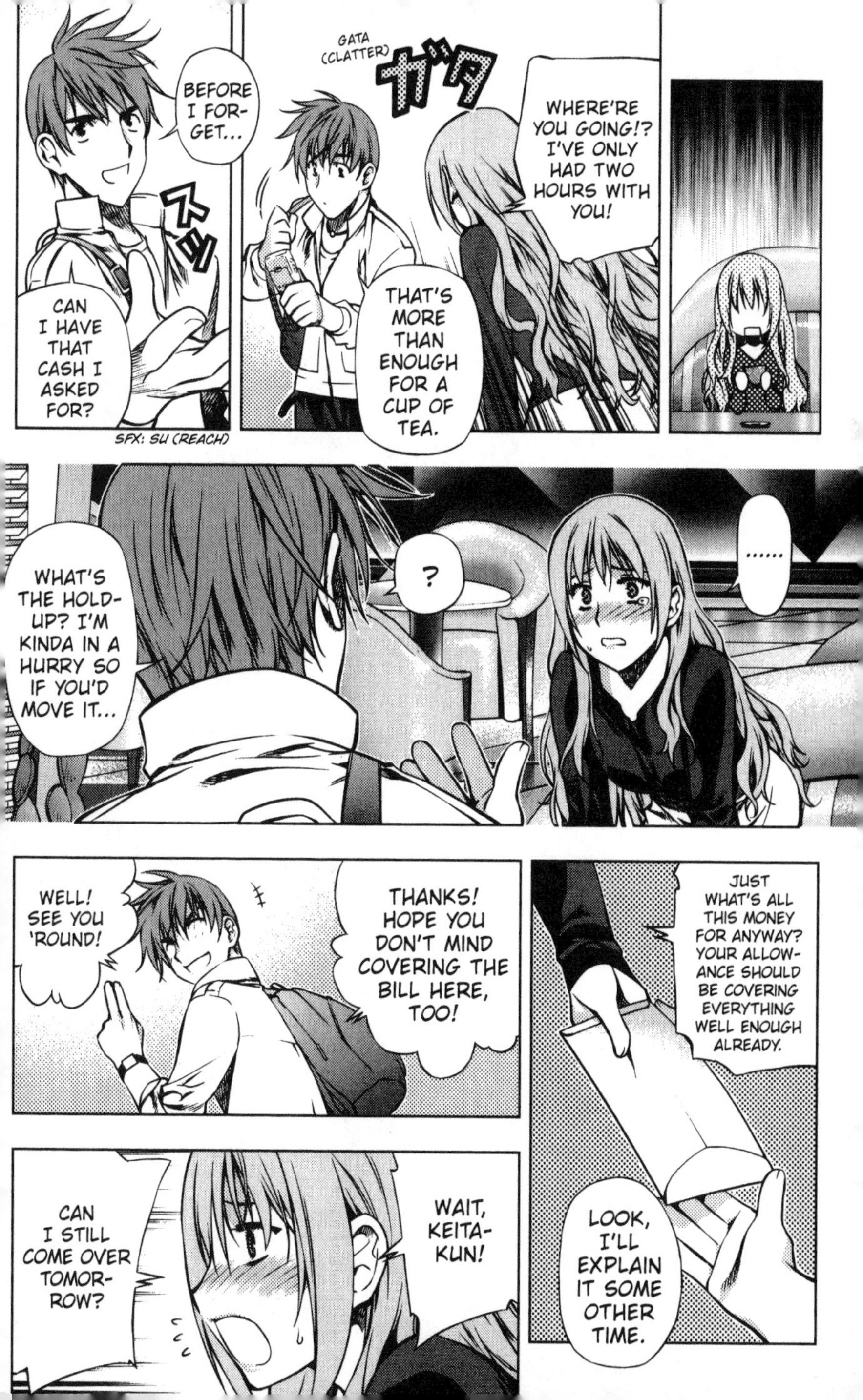
WHERE'RE YOU GOING!? I'VE ONLY HAD TWO HOURS WITH YOU!
GATA (CLATTER)
THAT'S MORE THAN ENOUGH FOR A CUP OF TEA.
BEFORE I FOR-GET...
CAN I HAVE THAT CASH I ASKED FOR?
SFX: SU (REACH)
......
?
WHAT'S THE HOLD-UP? I'M KINDA IN A HURRY SO IF YOU'D MOVE IT...
JUST WHAT'S ALL THIS MONEY FOR ANYWAY? YOUR ALLOW-ANCE SHOULD BE COVERING EVERYTHING WELL ENOUGH ALREADY.
LOOK, I'LL EXPLAIN IT SOME OTHER TIME.
THANKS! HOPE YOU DON'T MIND COVERING THE BILL HERE, TOO!
WELL! SEE YOU 'ROUND!
WAIT, KEITA-KUN!
CAN I STILL COME OVER TOMOR-ROW?

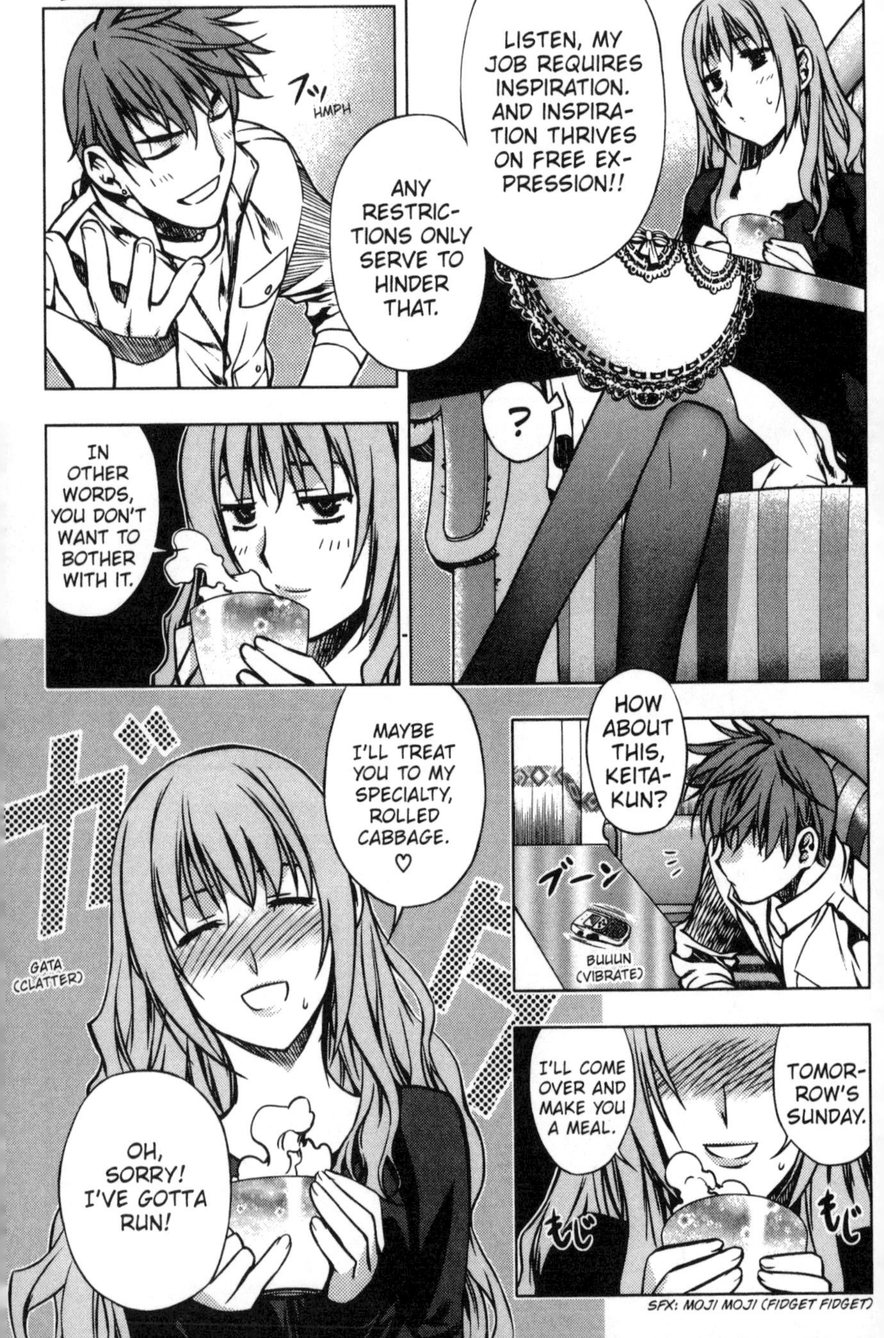
LISTEN, MY JOB REQUIRES INSPIRATION. AND INSPIRATION THRIVES ON FREE EXPRESSION!!
ANY RESTRICTIONS ONLY SERVE TO HINDER THAT.
?
HMPH
IN OTHER WORDS, YOU DON'T WANT TO BOTHER WITH IT.
HOW ABOUT THIS, KEITA-KUN?
BUUUN (VIBRATE)
TOMORROW'S SUNDAY.
I'LL COME OVER AND MAKE YOU A MEAL.
MAYBE I'LL TREAT YOU TO MY SPECIALTY, ROLLED CABBAGE. ♡
GATA (CLATTER)
OH, SORRY! I'VE GOTTA RUN!

SFX: MOJI MOJI (FIDGET FIDGET)

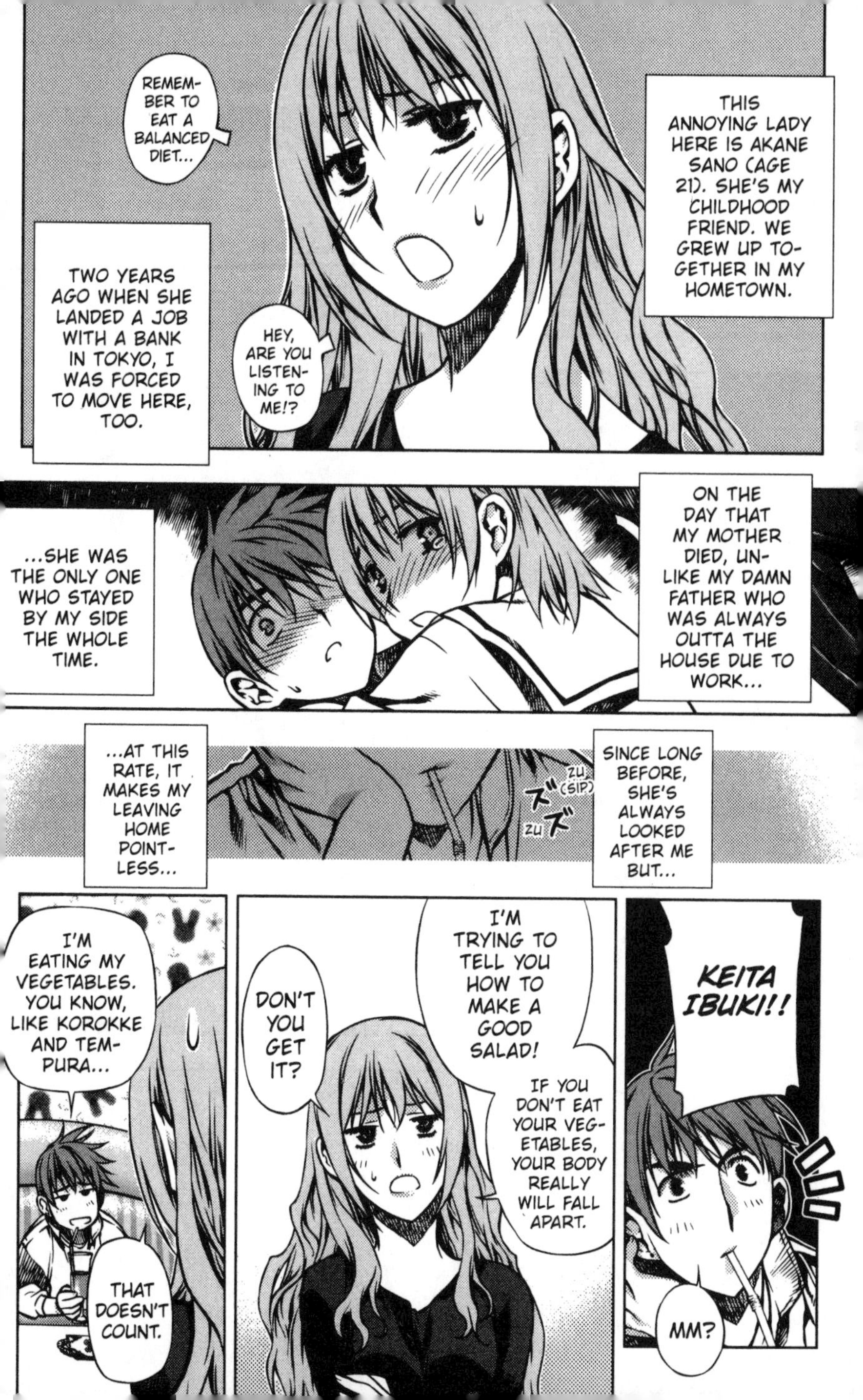
THIS ANNOYING LADY HERE IS AKANE SANO (AGE 21). SHE'S MY CHILDHOOD FRIEND. WE GREW UP TOGETHER IN MY HOMETOWN.
REMEMBER TO EAT A BALANCED DIET...
HEY, ARE YOU LISTENING TO ME!?
TWO YEARS AGO WHEN SHE LANDED A JOB WITH A BANK IN TOKYO, I WAS FORCED TO MOVE HERE, TOO.
ON THE DAY THAT MY MOTHER DIED, UNLIKE MY DAMN FATHER WHO WAS ALWAYS OUTTA THE HOUSE DUE TO WORK...
...SHE WAS THE ONLY ONE WHO STAYED BY MY SIDE THE WHOLE TIME.
SINCE LONG BEFORE, SHE'S ALWAYS LOOKED AFTER ME BUT...
ZU (SIP)
ZU
...AT THIS RATE, IT MAKES MY LEAVING HOME POINTLESS...
KEITA IBUKI!!
MM?
I'M TRYING TO TELL YOU HOW TO MAKE A GOOD SALAD!
DON'T YOU GET IT?
IF YOU DON'T EAT YOUR VEGETABLES, YOUR BODY REALLY WILL FALL APART.
I'M EATING MY VEGETABLES. YOU KNOW, LIKE KOROKKE AND TEMPURA...
THAT DOESN'T COUNT.

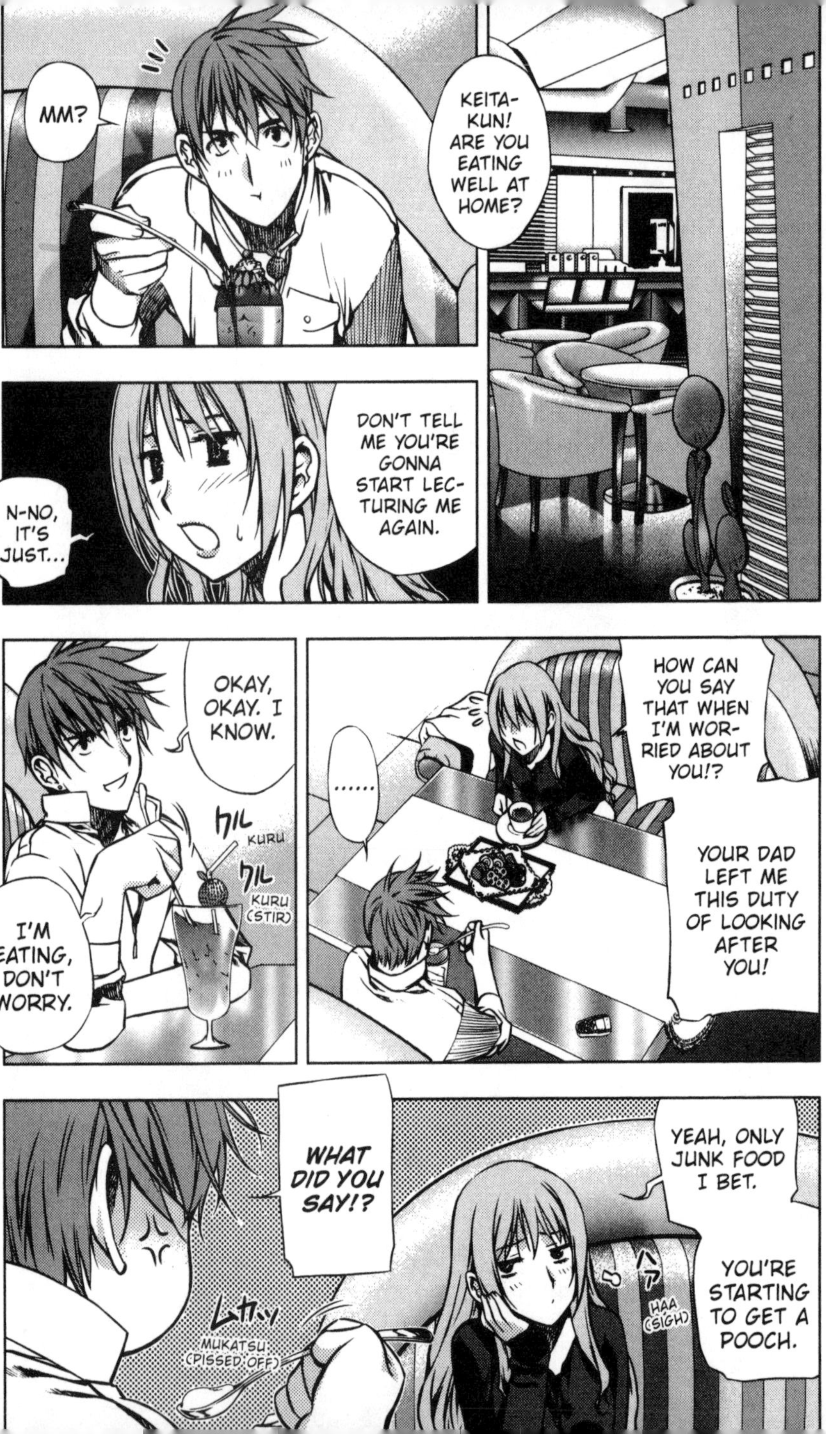
KEITA-KUN! ARE YOU EATING WELL AT HOME?
MM?
DON'T TELL ME YOU'RE GONNA START LEC-TURING ME AGAIN.
N-NO, IT'S JUST...
HOW CAN YOU SAY THAT WHEN I'M WOR-RIED ABOUT YOU!?
YOUR DAD LEFT ME THIS DUTY OF LOOKING AFTER YOU!
......
OKAY, OKAY. I KNOW.
クル KURU
クル KURU (STIR)
I'M EATING, DON'T WORRY.
YEAH, ONLY JUNK FOOD I BET.
YOU'RE STARTING TO GET A POOCH.
ハァ HAA (SIGH)
WHAT DID YOU SAY!?
ムカッ MUKATSU (PISSED OFF)

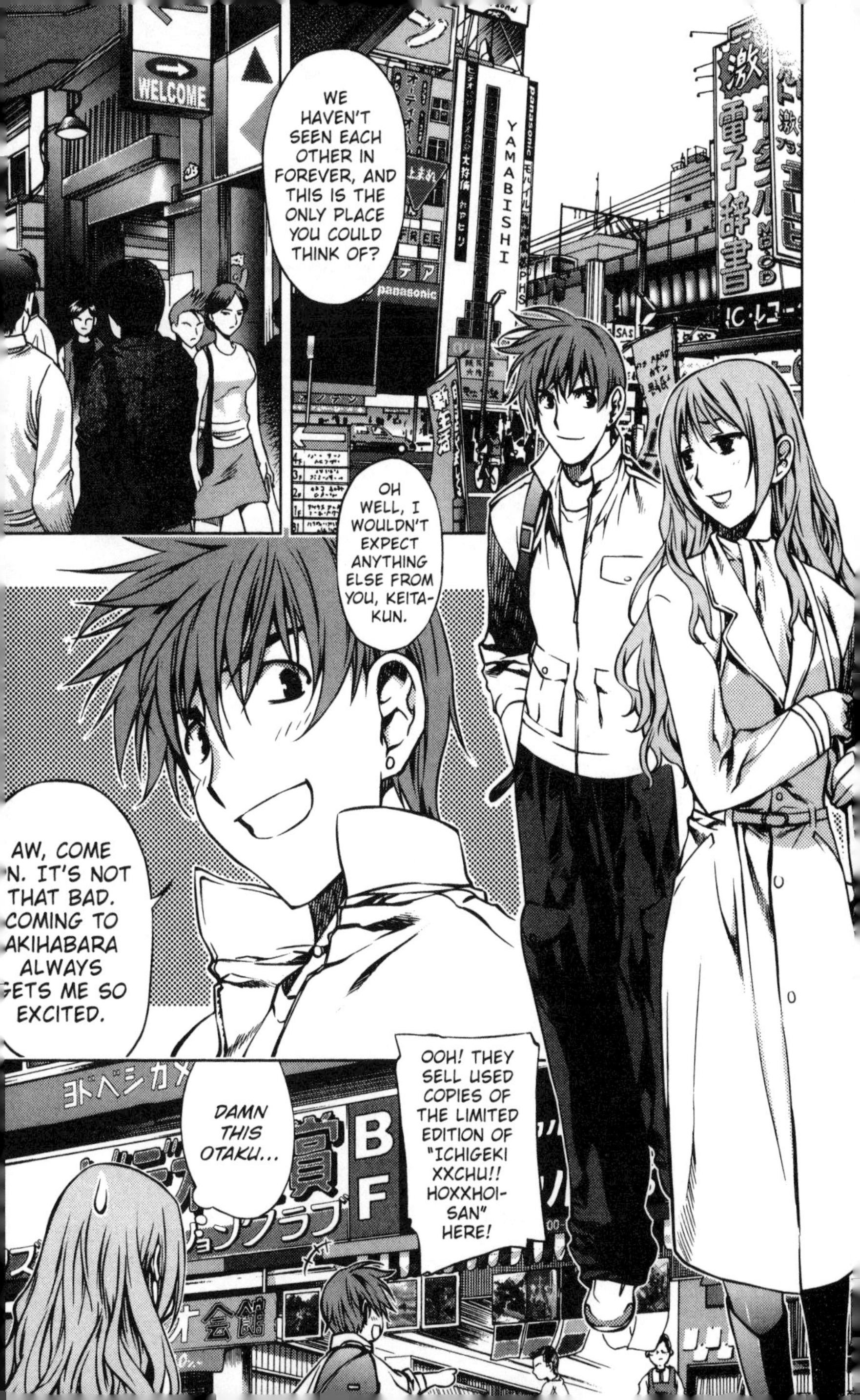
WELCOME
YAMABISHI
panasonic
WE HAVEN'T SEEN EACH OTHER IN FOREVER, AND THIS IS THE ONLY PLACE YOU COULD THINK OF?
OH WELL, I WOULDN'T EXPECT ANYTHING ELSE FROM YOU, KEITA-KUN.
AW, COME N. IT'S NOT THAT BAD. COMING TO AKIHABARA ALWAYS GETS ME SO EXCITED.
OOH! THEY SELL USED COPIES OF THE LIMITED EDITION OF "ICHIGEKI XXCHU!! HOXXHOI-SAN" HERE!
DAMN THIS OTAKU...

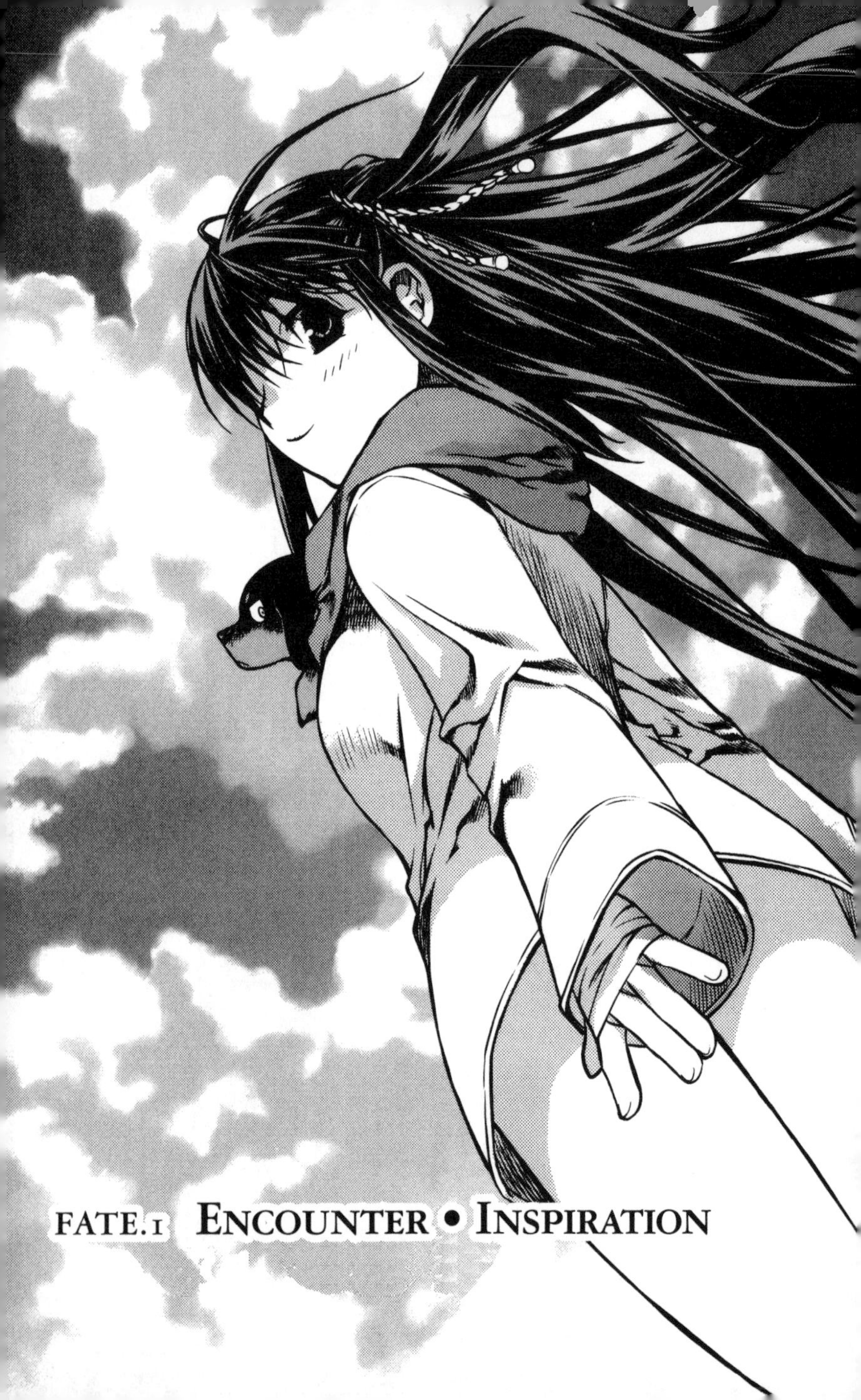

FATE.1 ENCOUNTER • INSPIRATION

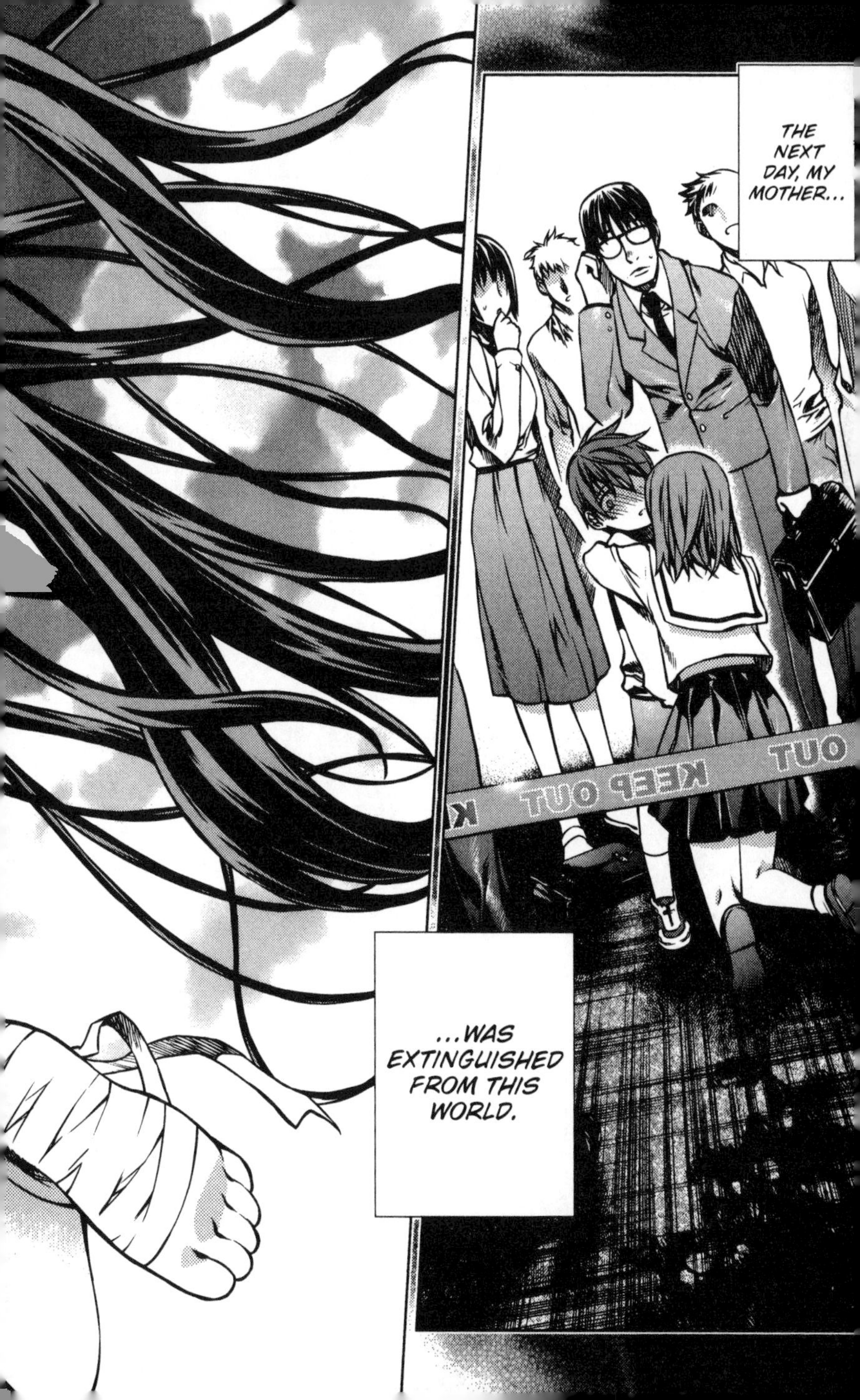
THE NEXT DAY, MY MOTHER...
KEEP OUT
...WAS EXTINGUISHED FROM THIS WORLD.

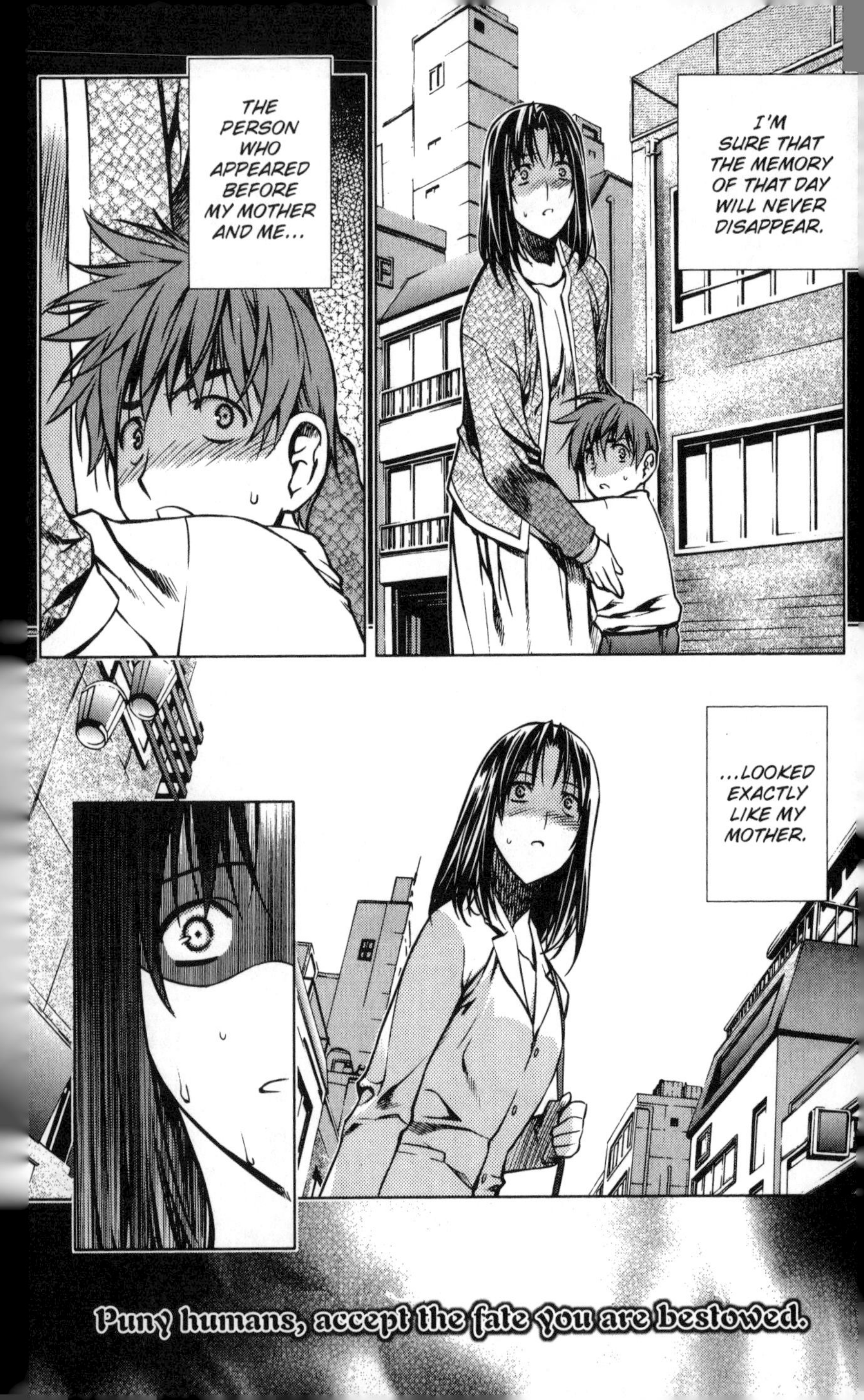
I'M SURE THAT THE MEMORY OF THAT DAY WILL NEVER DISAPPEAR.
THE PERSON WHO APPEARED BEFORE MY MOTHER AND ME...
...LOOKED EXACTLY LIKE MY MOTHER.
Puny humans, accept the fate you are bestowed.

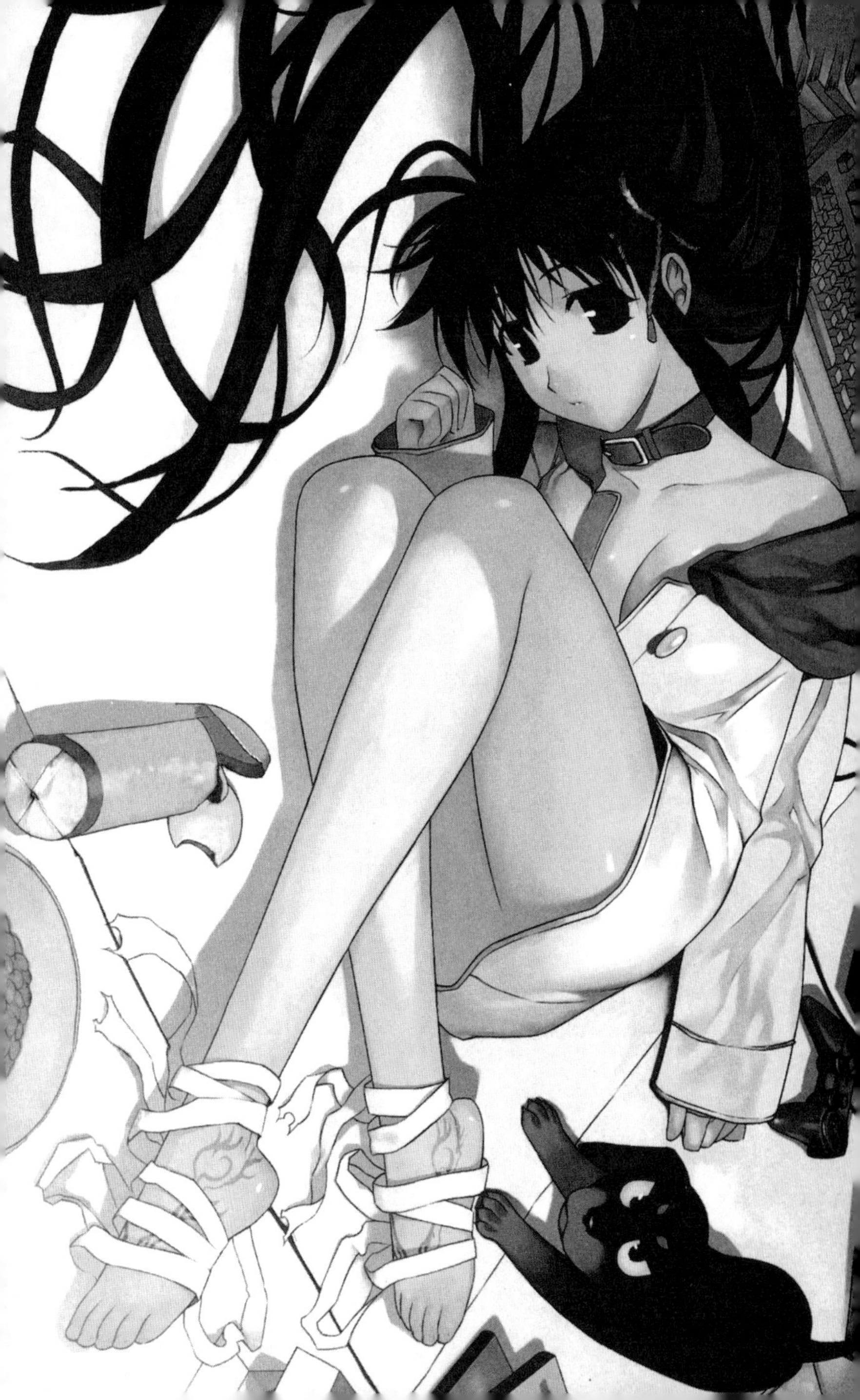

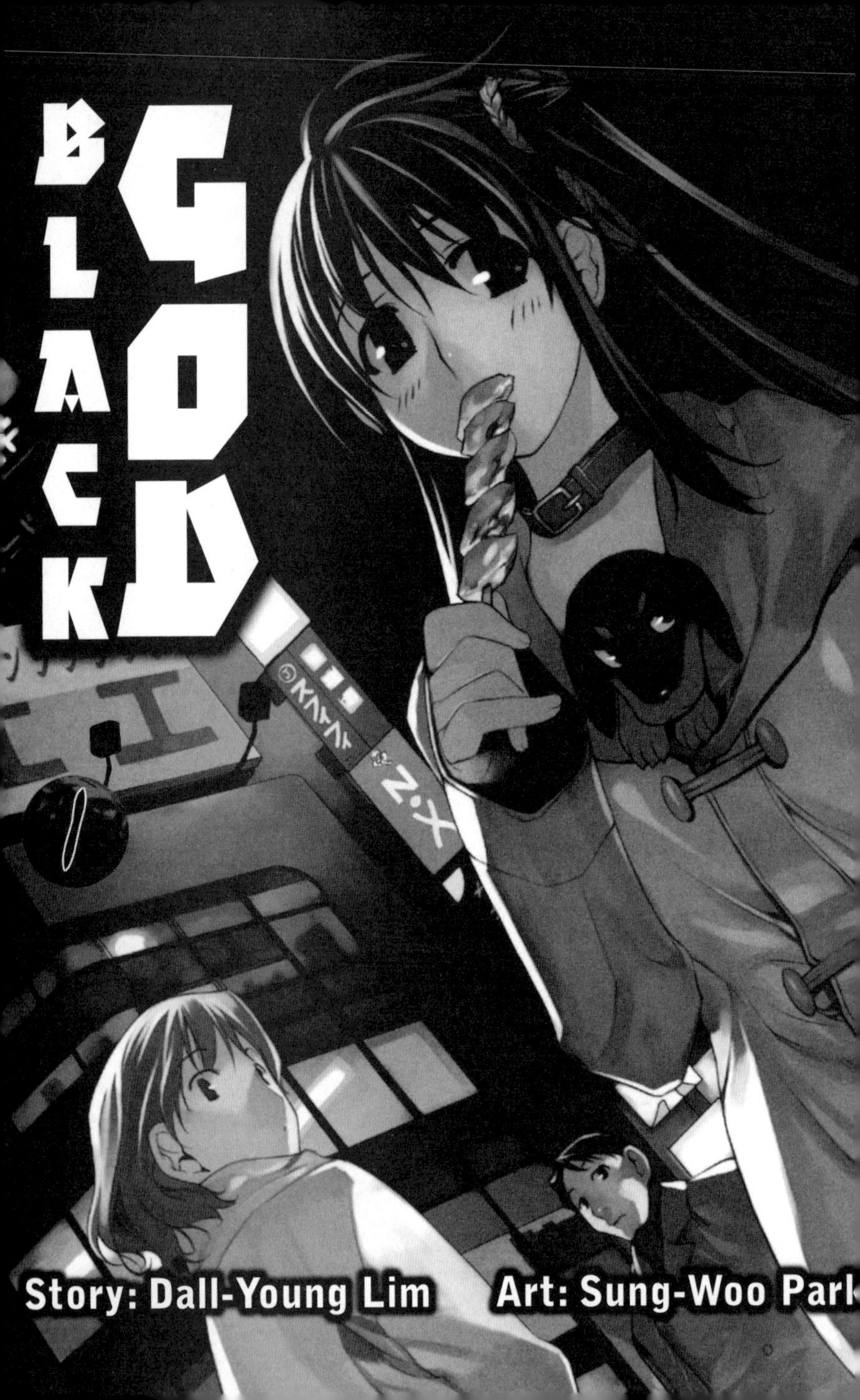
BLACK GOD
Story: Dall-Young Lim
Art: Sung-Woo Park

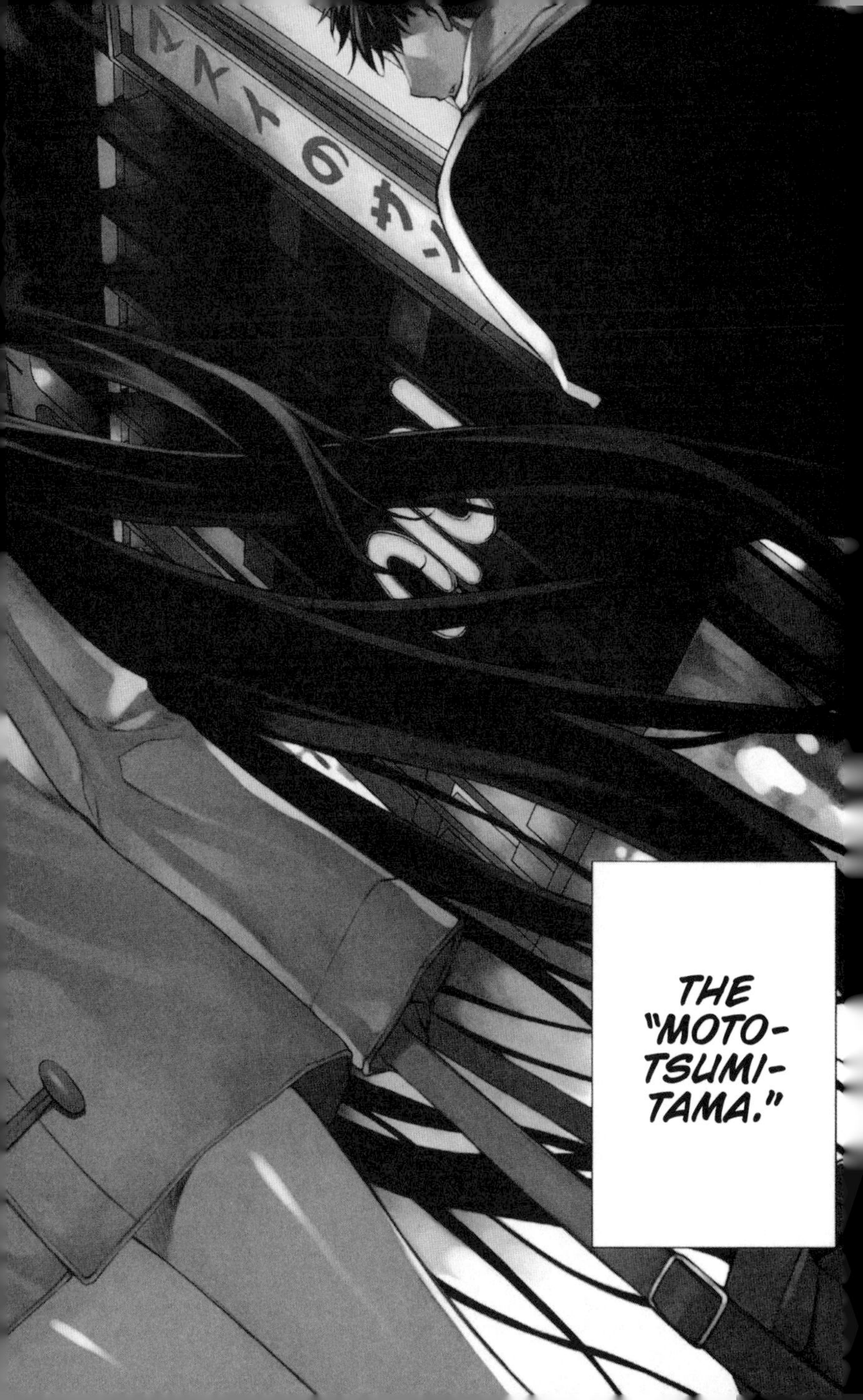
THE "MOTO-TSUMI-TAMA."

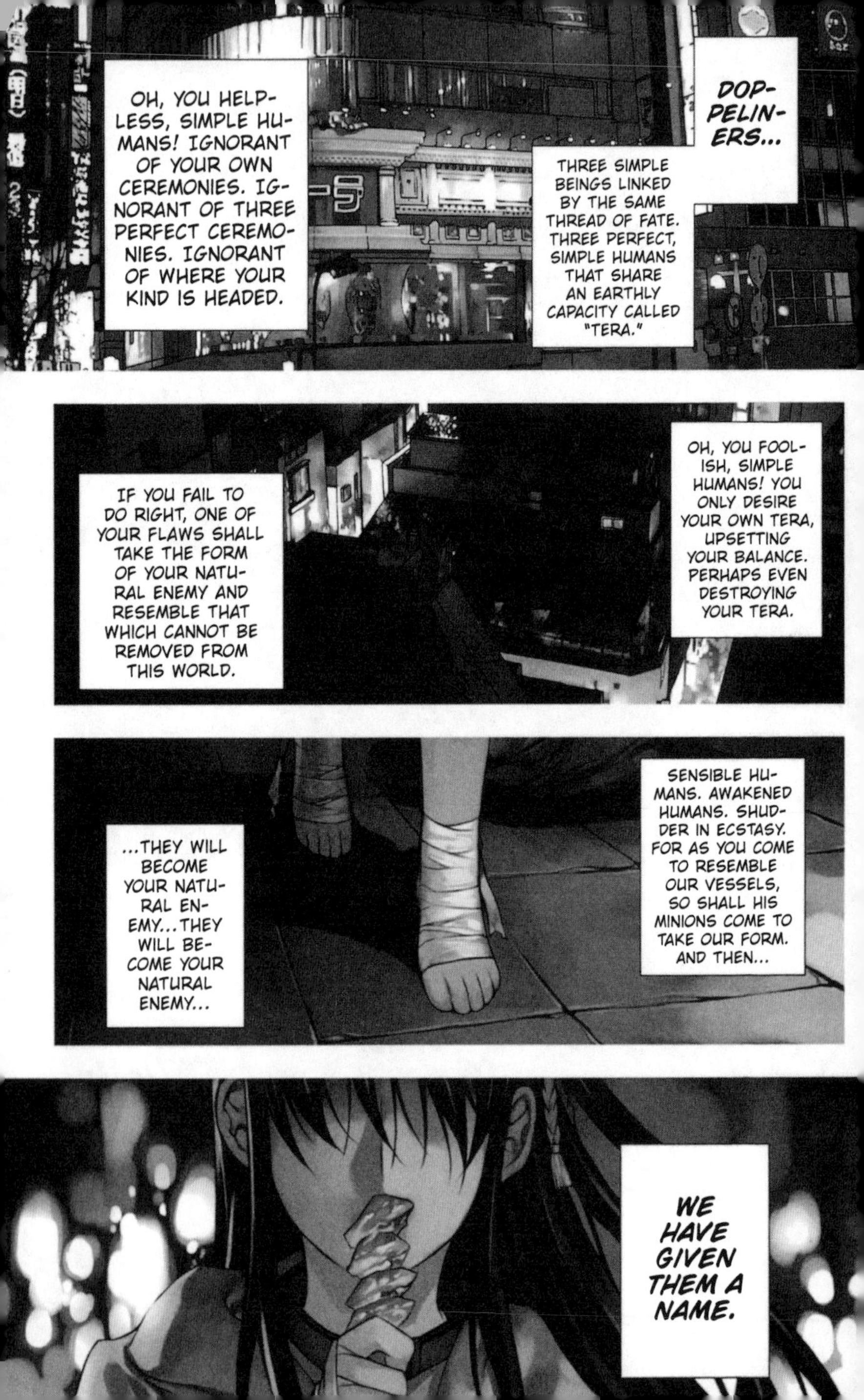
DOP-PELIN-ERS...
THREE SIMPLE BEINGS LINKED BY THE SAME THREAD OF FATE. THREE PERFECT, SIMPLE HUMANS THAT SHARE AN EARTHLY CAPACITY CALLED "TERA."
OH, YOU HELP-LESS, SIMPLE HU-MANS! IGNORANT OF YOUR OWN CEREMONIES. IG-NORANT OF THREE PERFECT CEREMO-NIES. IGNORANT OF WHERE YOUR KIND IS HEADED.
OH, YOU FOOL-ISH, SIMPLE HUMANS! YOU ONLY DESIRE YOUR OWN TERA, UPSETTING YOUR BALANCE. PERHAPS EVEN DESTROYING YOUR TERA.
IF YOU FAIL TO DO RIGHT, ONE OF YOUR FLAWS SHALL TAKE THE FORM OF YOUR NATU-RAL ENEMY AND RESEMBLE THAT WHICH CANNOT BE REMOVED FROM THIS WORLD.
SENSIBLE HU-MANS. AWAKENED HUMANS. SHUD-DER IN ECSTASY. FOR AS YOU COME TO RESEMBLE OUR VESSELS, SO SHALL HIS MINIONS COME TO TAKE OUR FORM. AND THEN...
...THEY WILL BECOME YOUR NATU-RAL EN-EMY...THEY WILL BE-COME YOUR NATURAL ENEMY...
WE HAVE GIVEN THEM A NAME.

BLACK GOD

Wending his way home after a bender one evening, master moocher and game programmer Keita Ibuki decides to satisfy a craving for ramen at a noodle stand. Instead of slurping soup, though, he surrenders his meal to a manic girl who (unbeknownst to Keita) is a Mototsumitama, a guardian of the "coexistence equilibrium." When his new acquaintance is attacked, Keita gets caught in the crossfire and loses an arm. Awakening from the shock of his injury, Keita finds himself back in his apartment–arm intact! But whose arm is it?! Asking the strange girl raiding his refrigerator only reveals that Keita's life has become a great deal more complicated...

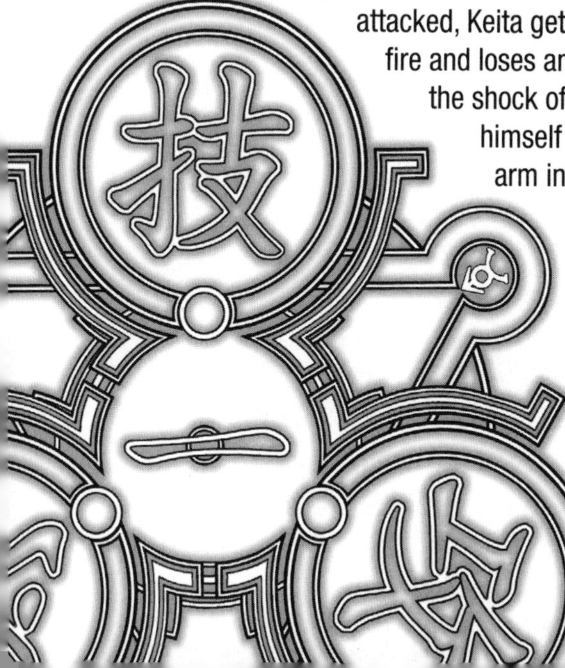
技
一

What happens when you lose an arm and gain another... only to
discover there's still a warm body attached?!

- ISBN-13: 978-0-7595-2349-4
- ISBN-10: 0-7595-2349-5
- $10.99 USD/$12.75 CAN/£5.99 UK
- October 2007

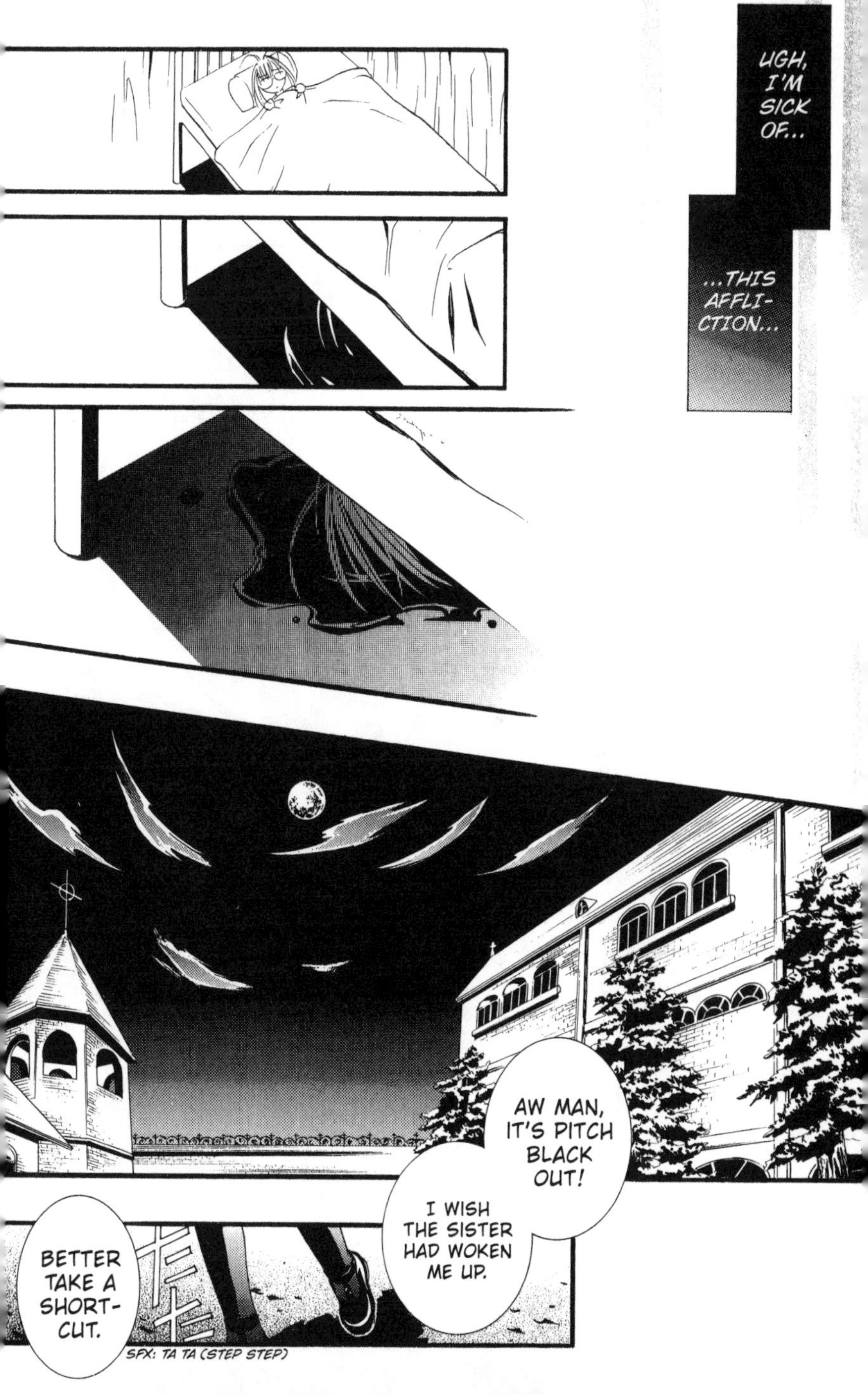
UGH, I'M SICK OF...
...THIS AFFLICTION...
AW MAN, IT'S PITCH BLACK OUT!
I WISH THE SISTER HAD WOKEN ME UP.
BETTER TAKE A SHORT-CUT.
SFX: TA TA (STEP STEP)

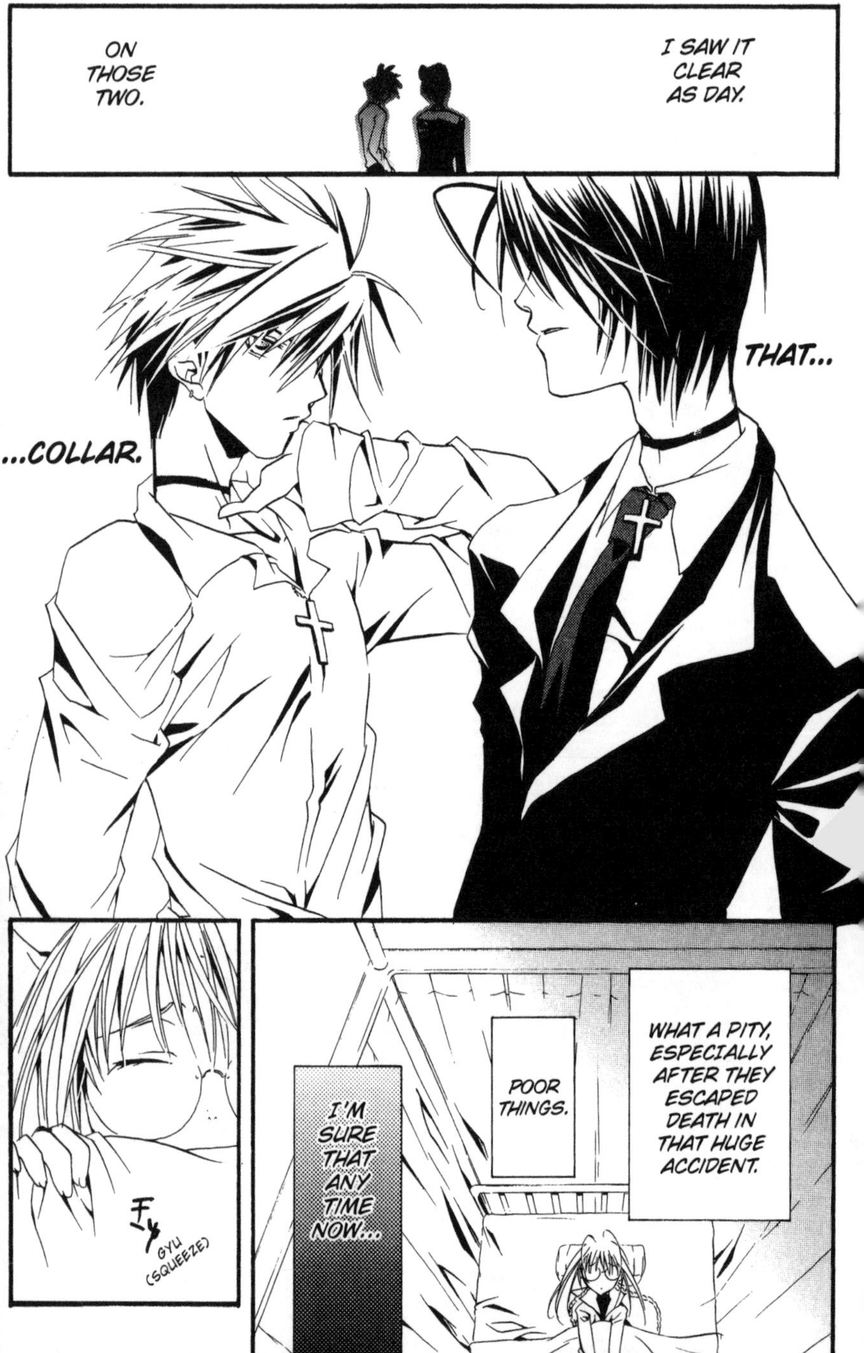
I SAW IT CLEAR AS DAY.
ON THOSE TWO.
THAT...
...COLLAR.
WHAT A PITY, ESPECIALLY AFTER THEY ESCAPED DEATH IN THAT HUGE ACCIDENT.
POOR THINGS.
I'M SURE THAT ANY TIME NOW...
GYU (SQUEEZE)

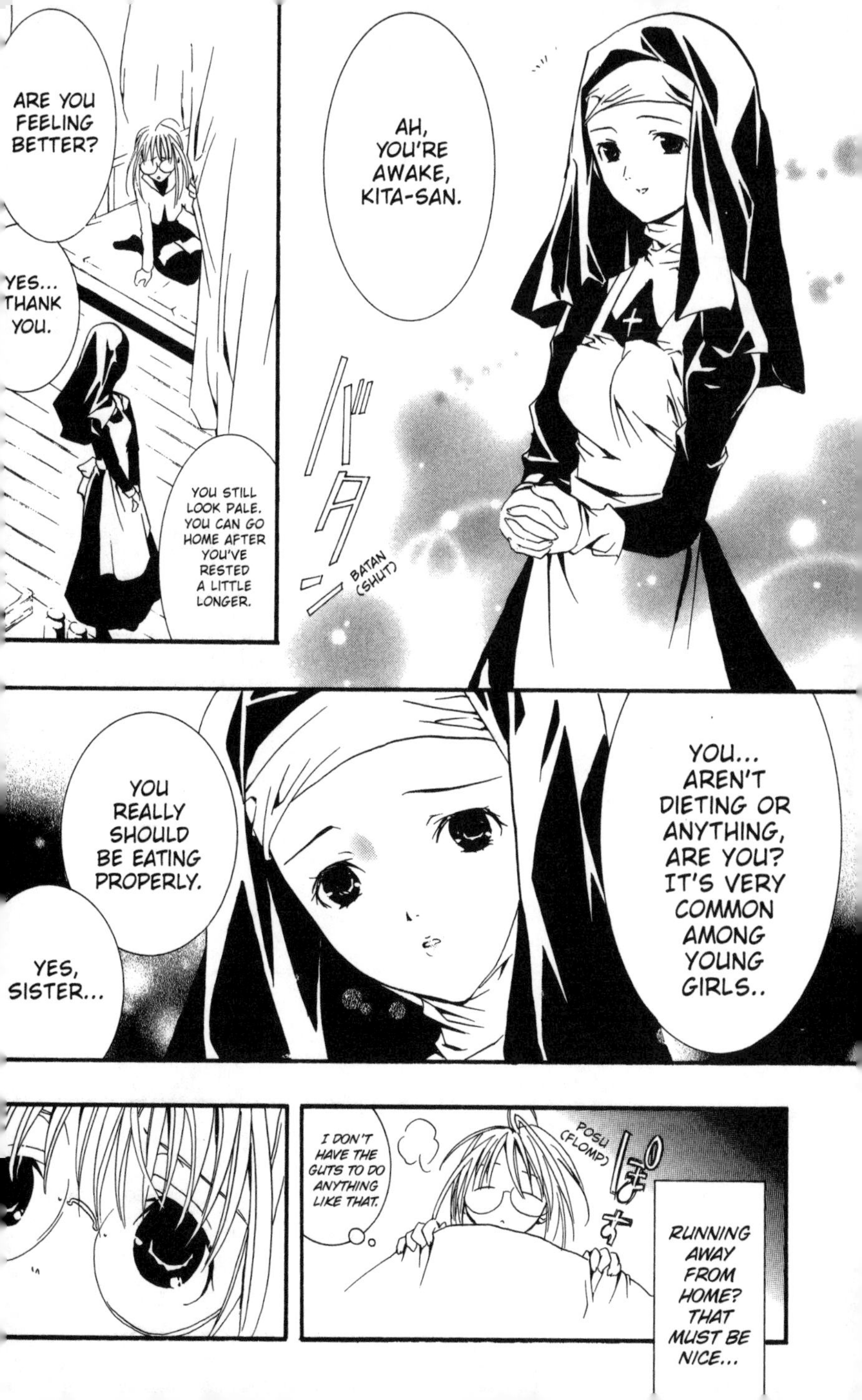
AH, YOU'RE AWAKE, KITA-SAN.
BATAN (SHUT)
ARE YOU FEELING BETTER?
YES... THANK YOU.
YOU STILL LOOK PALE. YOU CAN GO HOME AFTER YOU'VE RESTED A LITTLE LONGER.
YOU... AREN'T DIETING OR ANYTHING, ARE YOU? IT'S VERY COMMON AMONG YOUNG GIRLS..
YOU REALLY SHOULD BE EATING PROPERLY.
YES, SISTER...
ぽす
POSU (FLOMP)
RUNNING AWAY FROM HOME? THAT MUST BE NICE...
I DON'T HAVE THE GUTS TO DO ANYTHING LIKE THAT.

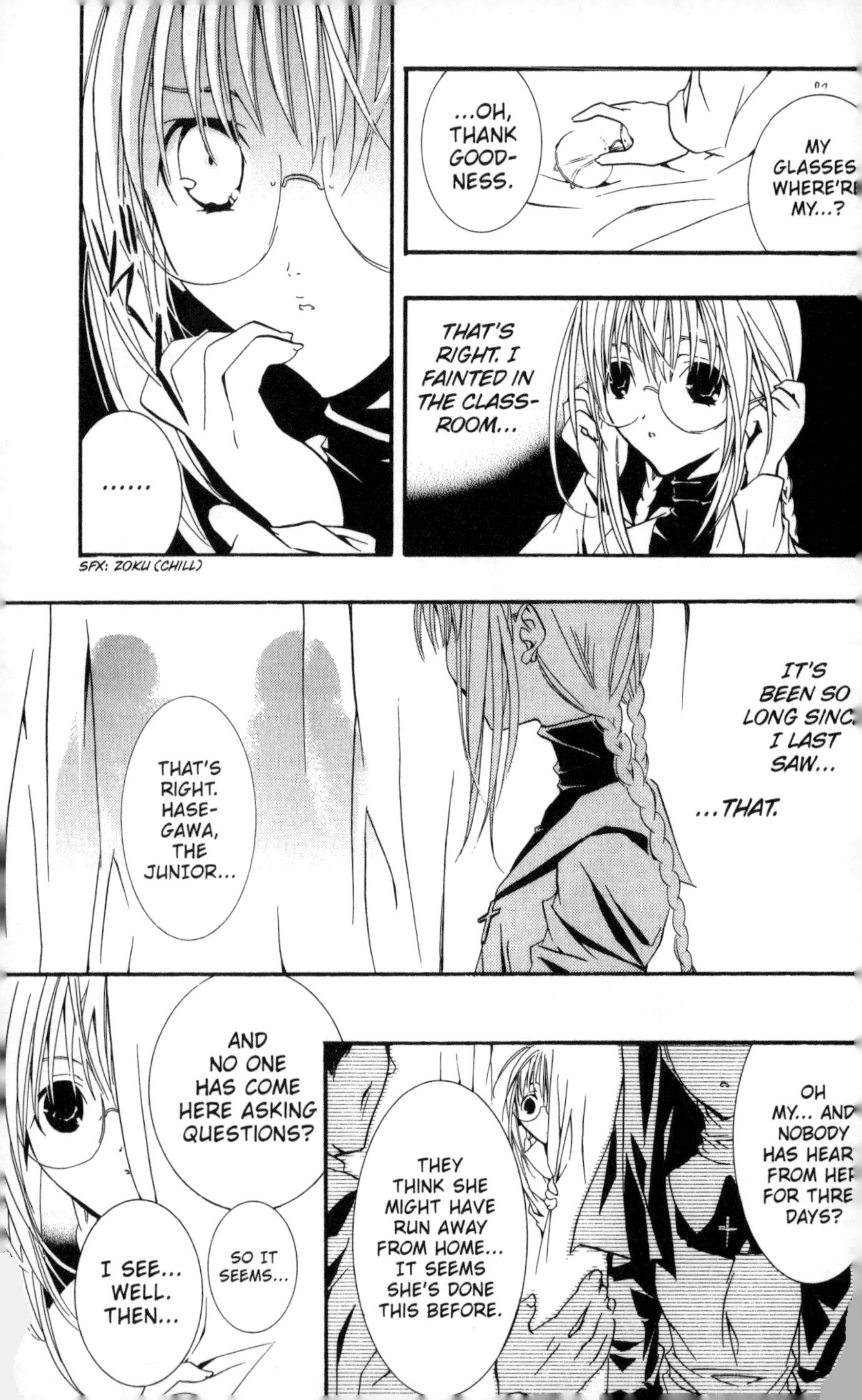
MY GLASSES WHERE'R MY...?
...OH, THANK GOODNESS.
THAT'S RIGHT. I FAINTED IN THE CLASSROOM...
......
SFX: ZOKU (CHILL)
IT'S BEEN SO LONG SINC I LAST SAW...
...THAT.
THAT'S RIGHT. HASEGAWA, THE JUNIOR...
OH MY... AND NOBODY HAS HEAR FROM HE FOR THRE DAYS?
THEY THINK SHE MIGHT HAVE RUN AWAY FROM HOME... IT SEEMS SHE'S DONE THIS BEFORE.
AND NO ONE HAS COME HERE ASKING QUESTIONS?
SO IT SEEMS...
I SEE... WELL. THEN...

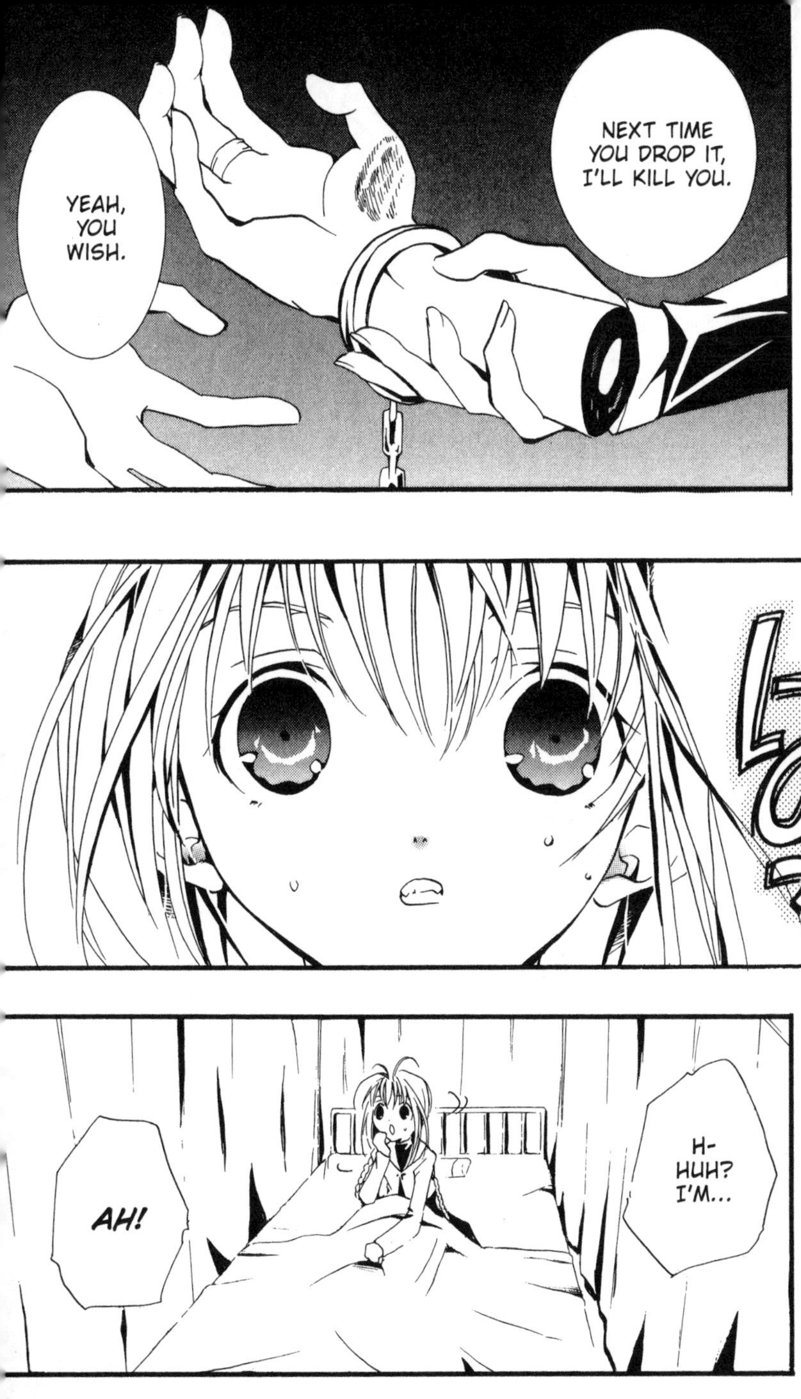
NEXT TIME YOU DROP IT, I'LL KILL YOU.
YEAH, YOU WISH.
はっ
HA (GASP)
H-HUH? I'M...
AH!

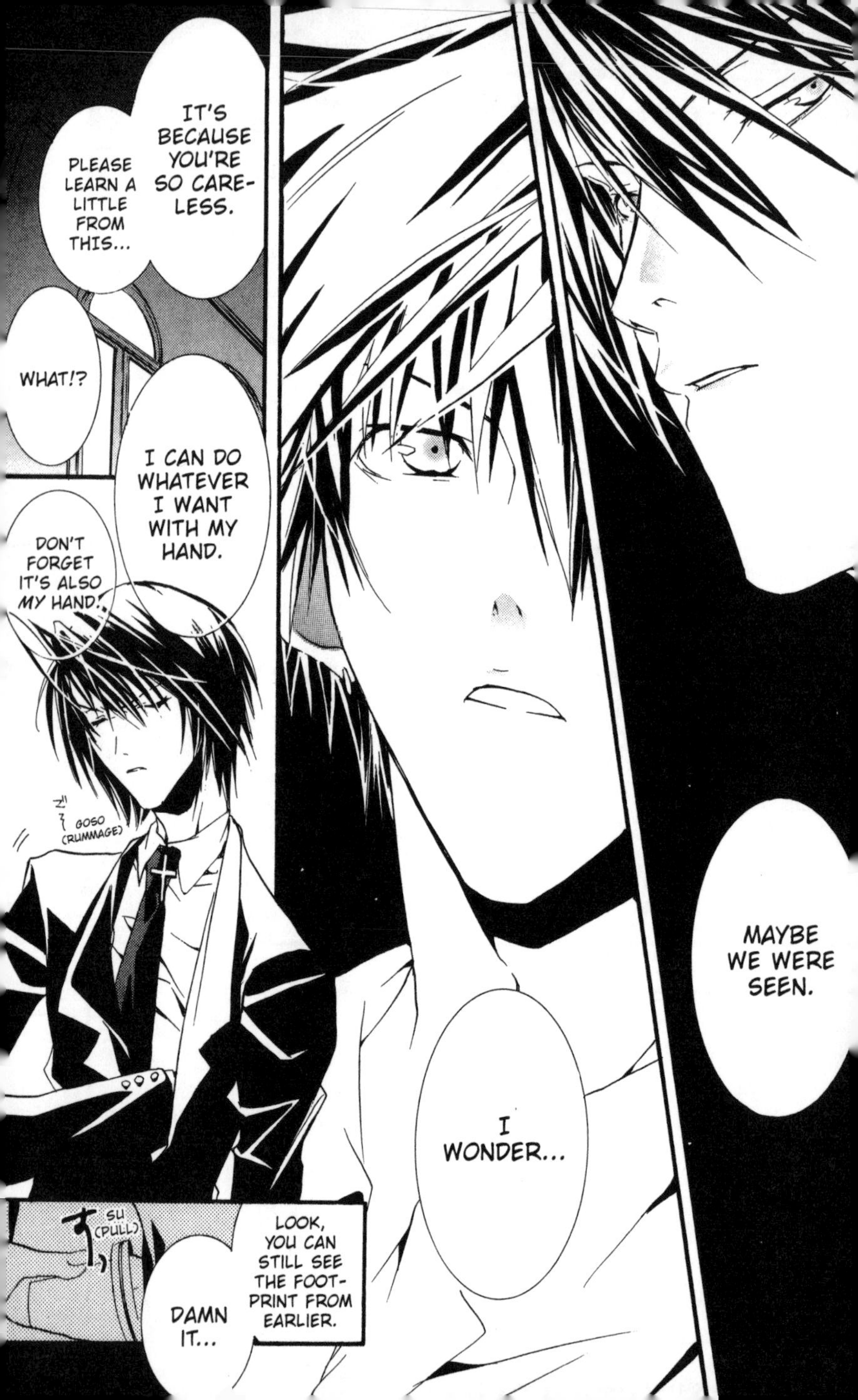
MAYBE WE WERE SEEN.
I WONDER...
IT'S BECAUSE YOU'RE SO CARE-LESS.
PLEASE LEARN A LITTLE FROM THIS...
WHAT!?
I CAN DO WHATEVER I WANT WITH MY HAND.
DON'T FORGET IT'S ALSO MY HAND!
GOSO (RUMMAGE)
SU (PULL)
LOOK, YOU CAN STILL SEE THE FOOT-PRINT FROM EARLIER.
DAMN IT...

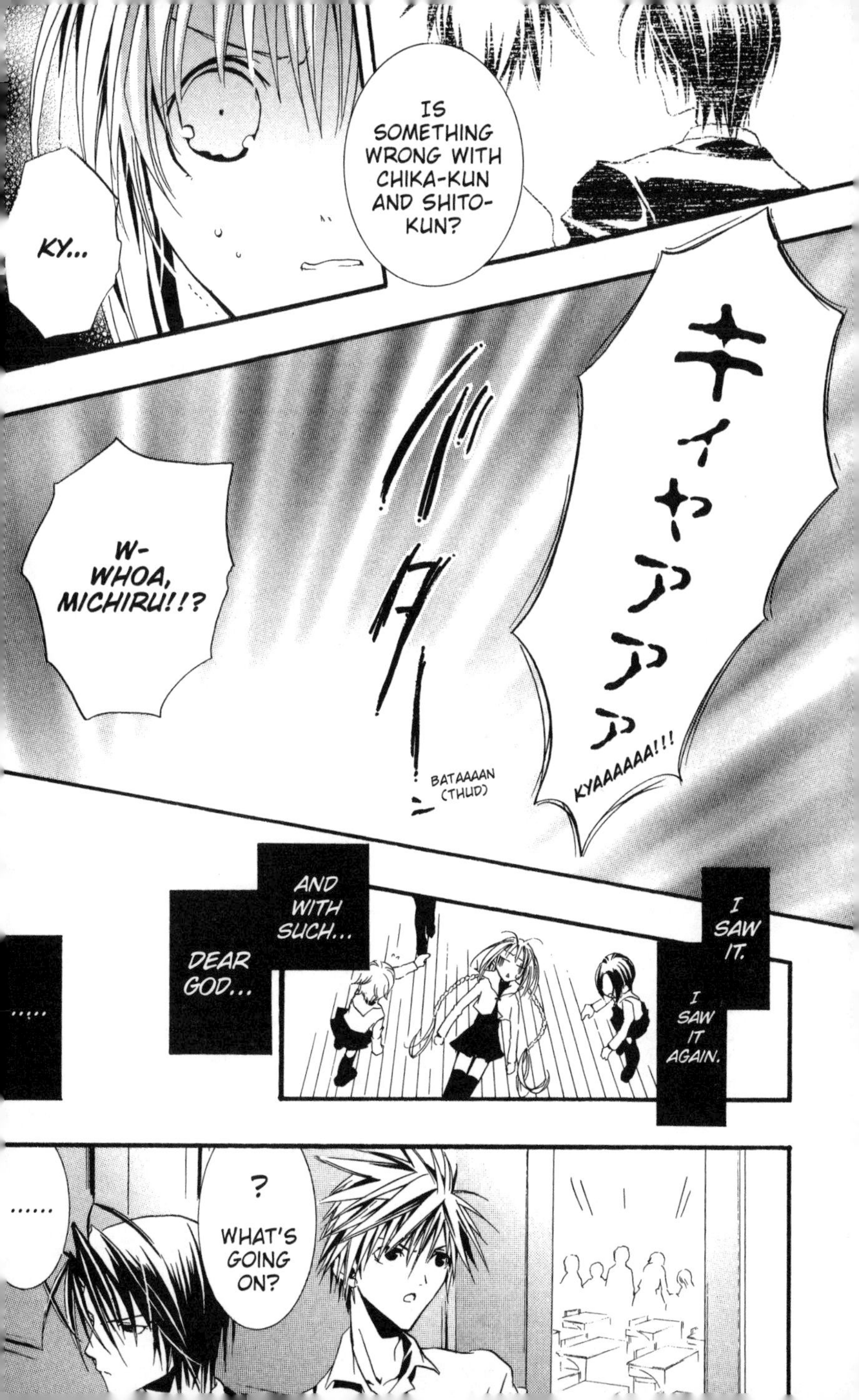
IS SOMETHING WRONG WITH CHIKA-KUN AND SHITO-KUN?
KY...
キイやアアア
KYAAAAAA!!!
バターン
BATAAAAN (THUD)
W-WHOA, MICHIRU!!?
I SAW IT.
I SAW IT AGAIN.
AND WITH SUCH...
DEAR GOD...
......
?
WHAT'S GOING ON?
......

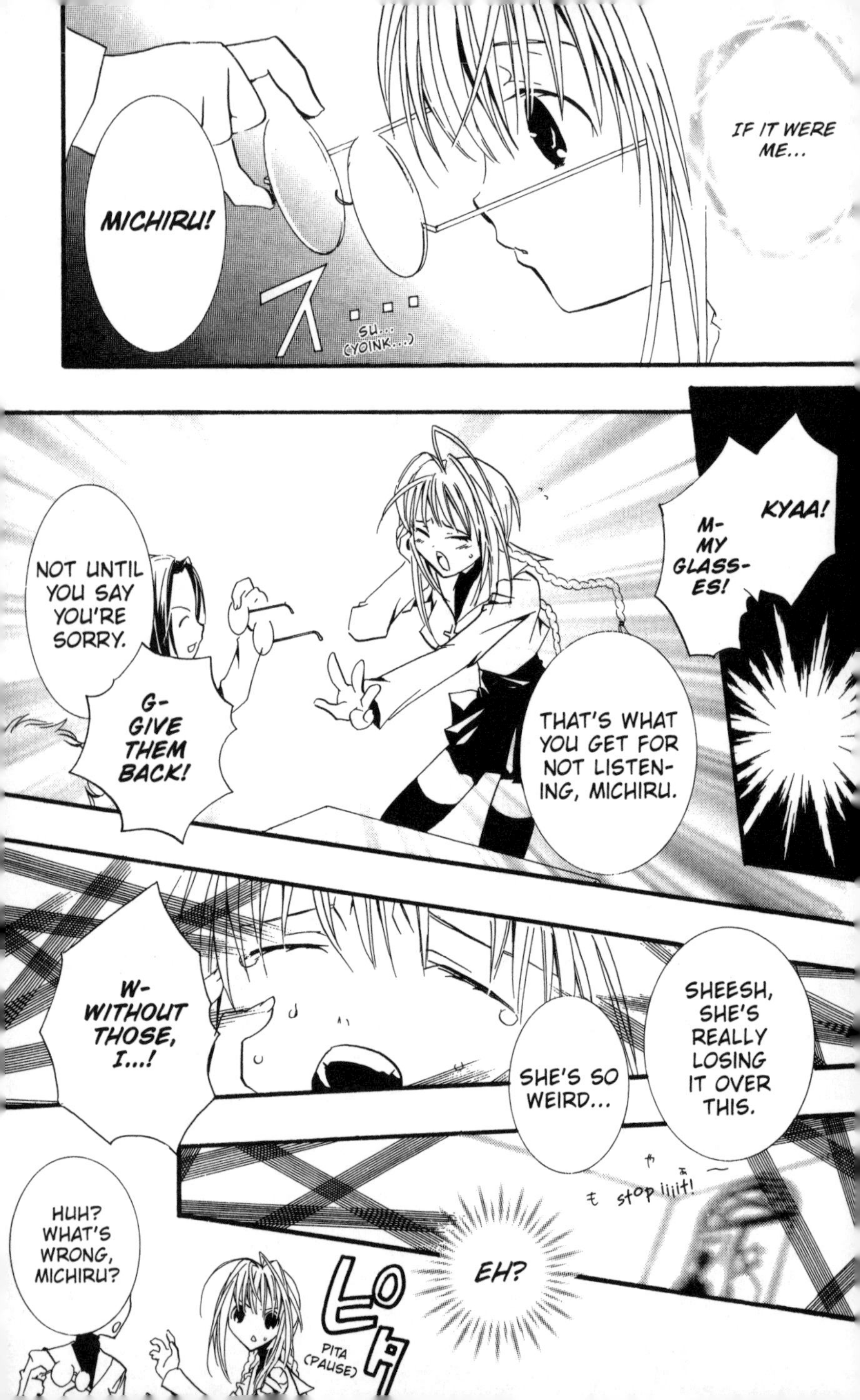
IF IT WERE ME...
MICHIRU!
SU... (YOINK...)
KYAA!
M-MY GLASSES!
THAT'S WHAT YOU GET FOR NOT LISTENING, MICHIRU.
NOT UNTIL YOU SAY YOU'RE SORRY.
G-GIVE THEM BACK!
SHEESH, SHE'S REALLY LOSING IT OVER THIS.
SHE'S SO WEIRD...
W-WITHOUT THOSE, I...!
stop iiiit!
EH?
PITA (PAUSE)
HUH? WHAT'S WRONG, MICHIRU?

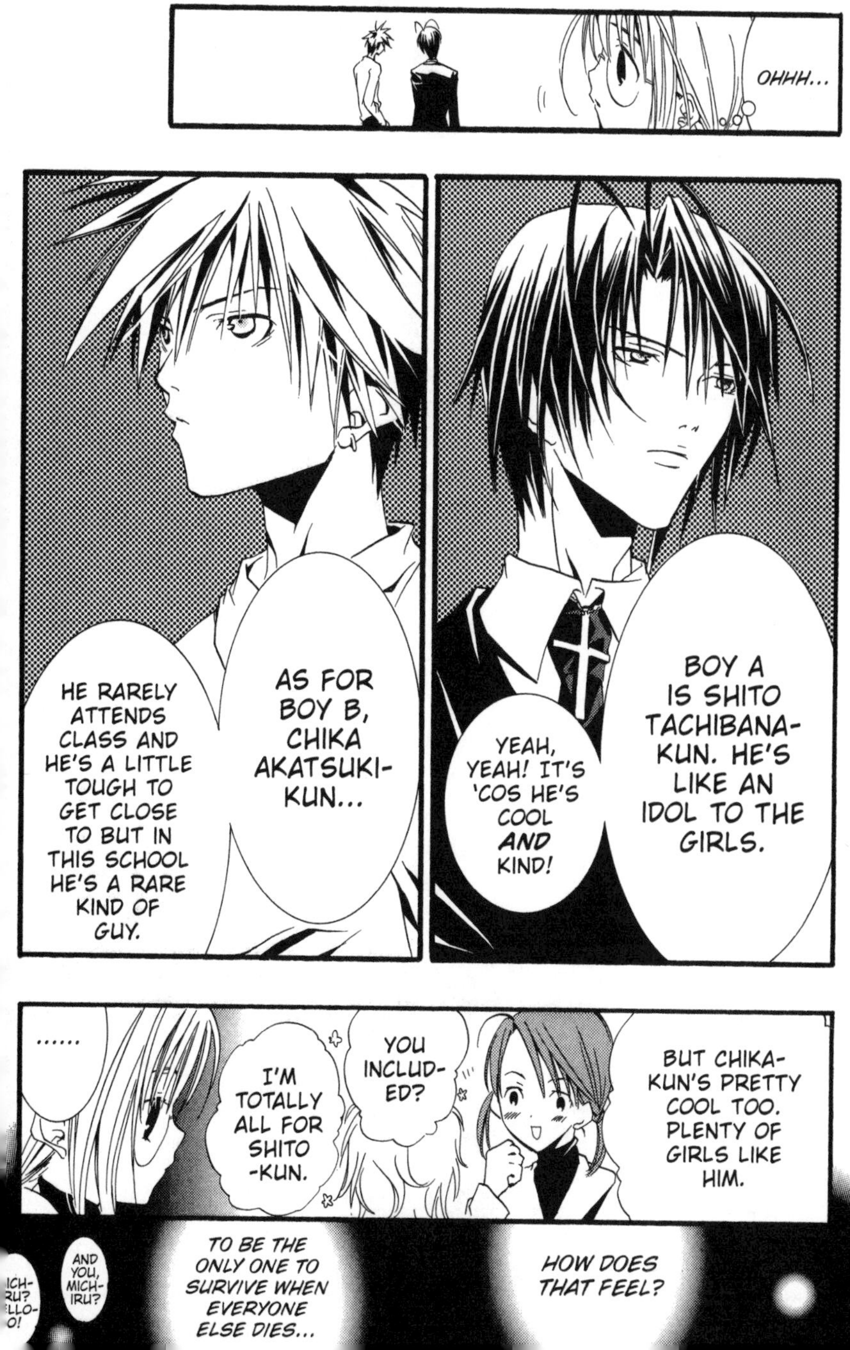

OHHH...
BOY A IS SHITO TACHIBANA-KUN. HE'S LIKE AN IDOL TO THE GIRLS.
YEAH, YEAH! IT'S 'COS HE'S COOL *AND* KIND!
AS FOR BOY B, CHIKA AKATSUKI-KUN...
HE RARELY ATTENDS CLASS AND HE'S A LITTLE TOUGH TO GET CLOSE TO BUT IN THIS SCHOOL HE'S A RARE KIND OF GUY.
BUT CHIKA-KUN'S PRETTY COOL TOO. PLENTY OF GIRLS LIKE HIM.
YOU INCLUD-ED?
I'M TOTALLY ALL FOR SHITO-KUN.
......
HOW DOES THAT FEEL?
TO BE THE ONLY ONE TO SURVIVE WHEN EVERYONE ELSE DIES...
AND YOU, MICH-IRU?
ICH-RU? ELLO-O!

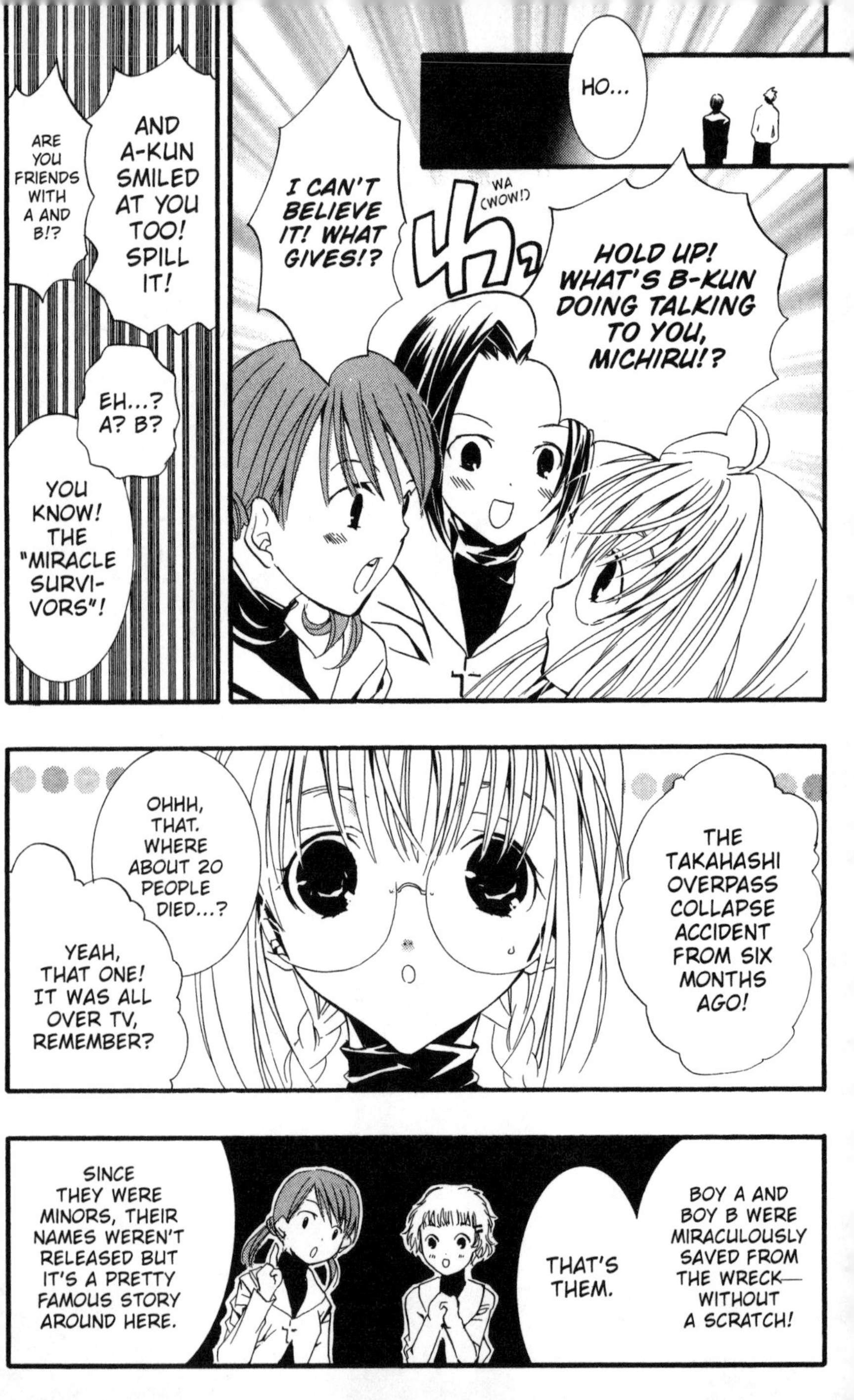
HO...
WA (WOW!)
HOLD UP! WHAT'S B-KUN DOING TALKING TO YOU, MICHIRU!?
I CAN'T BELIEVE IT! WHAT GIVES!?
AND A-KUN SMILED AT YOU TOO! SPILL IT!
ARE YOU FRIENDS WITH A AND B!?
EH...? A? B?
YOU KNOW! THE "MIRACLE SURVIVORS"!
THE TAKAHASHI OVERPASS COLLAPSE ACCIDENT FROM SIX MONTHS AGO!
OHHH, THAT. WHERE ABOUT 20 PEOPLE DIED...?
YEAH, THAT ONE! IT WAS ALL OVER TV, REMEMBER?
BOY A AND BOY B WERE MIRACULOUSLY SAVED FROM THE WRECK— WITHOUT A SCRATCH!
THAT'S THEM.
SINCE THEY WERE MINORS, THEIR NAMES WEREN'T RELEASED BUT IT'S A PRETTY FAMOUS STORY AROUND HERE.

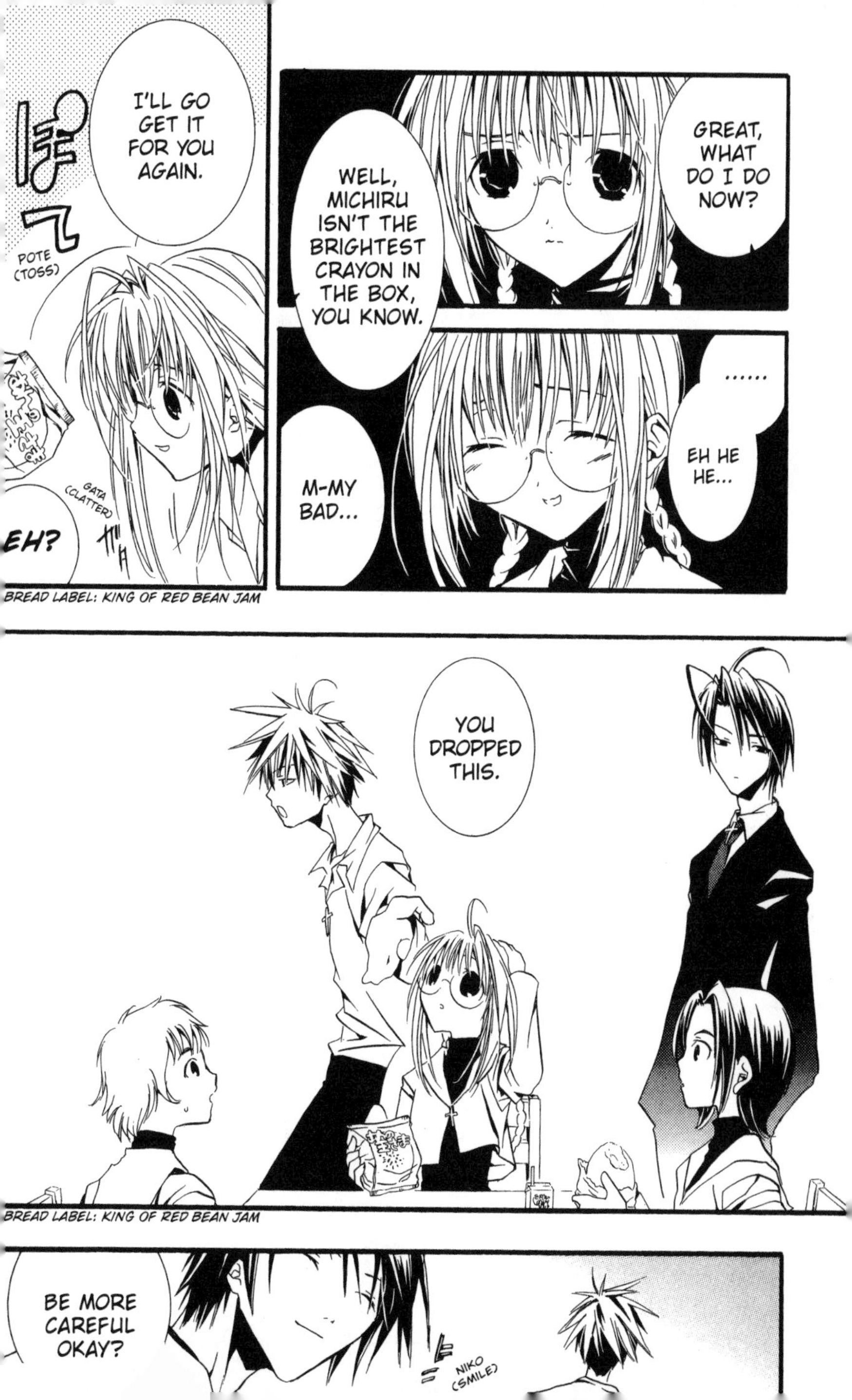
GREAT, WHAT DO I DO NOW?
WELL, MICHIRU ISN'T THE BRIGHTEST CRAYON IN THE BOX, YOU KNOW.
......
EH HE HE...
M-MY BAD...
I'LL GO GET IT FOR YOU AGAIN.
POTE (TOSS)
GATA (CLATTER)
EH?
BREAD LABEL: KING OF RED BEAN JAM
YOU DROPPED THIS.
BREAD LABEL: KING OF RED BEAN JAM
BE MORE CAREFUL OKAY?
NIKO (SMILE)

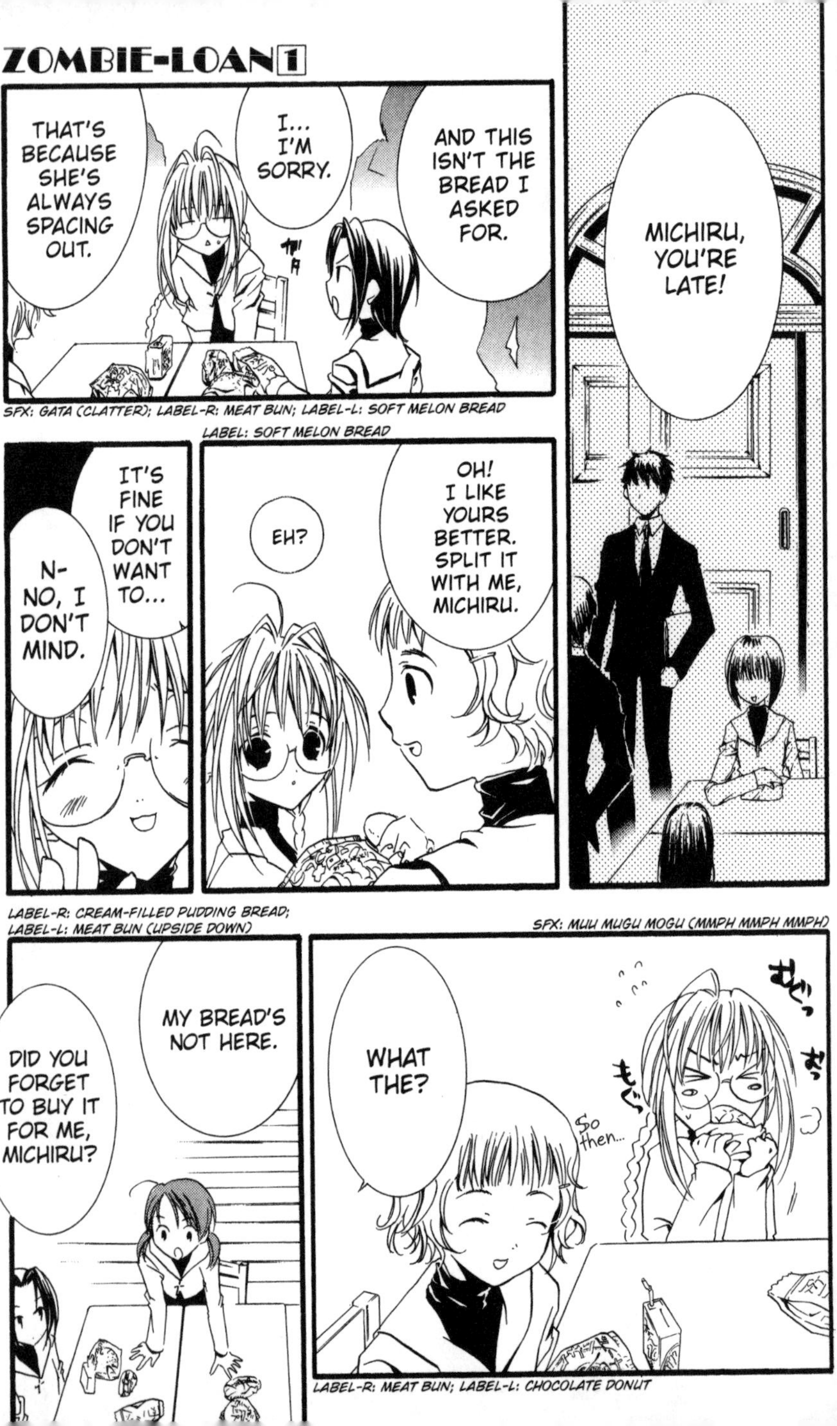
MICHIRU, YOU'RE LATE!
AND THIS ISN'T THE BREAD I ASKED FOR.
I... I'M SORRY.
THAT'S BECAUSE SHE'S ALWAYS SPACING OUT.
SFX: GATA (CLATTER); LABEL-R: MEAT BUN; LABEL-L: SOFT MELON BREAD
LABEL: SOFT MELON BREAD
OH! I LIKE YOURS BETTER. SPLIT IT WITH ME, MICHIRU.
EH?
IT'S FINE IF YOU DON'T WANT TO...
N-NO, I DON'T MIND.
SFX: MUU MUGU MOGU (MMPH MMPH MMPH)
LABEL-R: CREAM-FILLED PUDDING BREAD; LABEL-L: MEAT BUN (UPSIDE DOWN)
WHAT THE?
So then...
LABEL-R: MEAT BUN; LABEL-L: CHOCOLATE DONUT
MY BREAD'S NOT HERE.
DID YOU FORGET TO BUY IT FOR ME, MICHIRU?

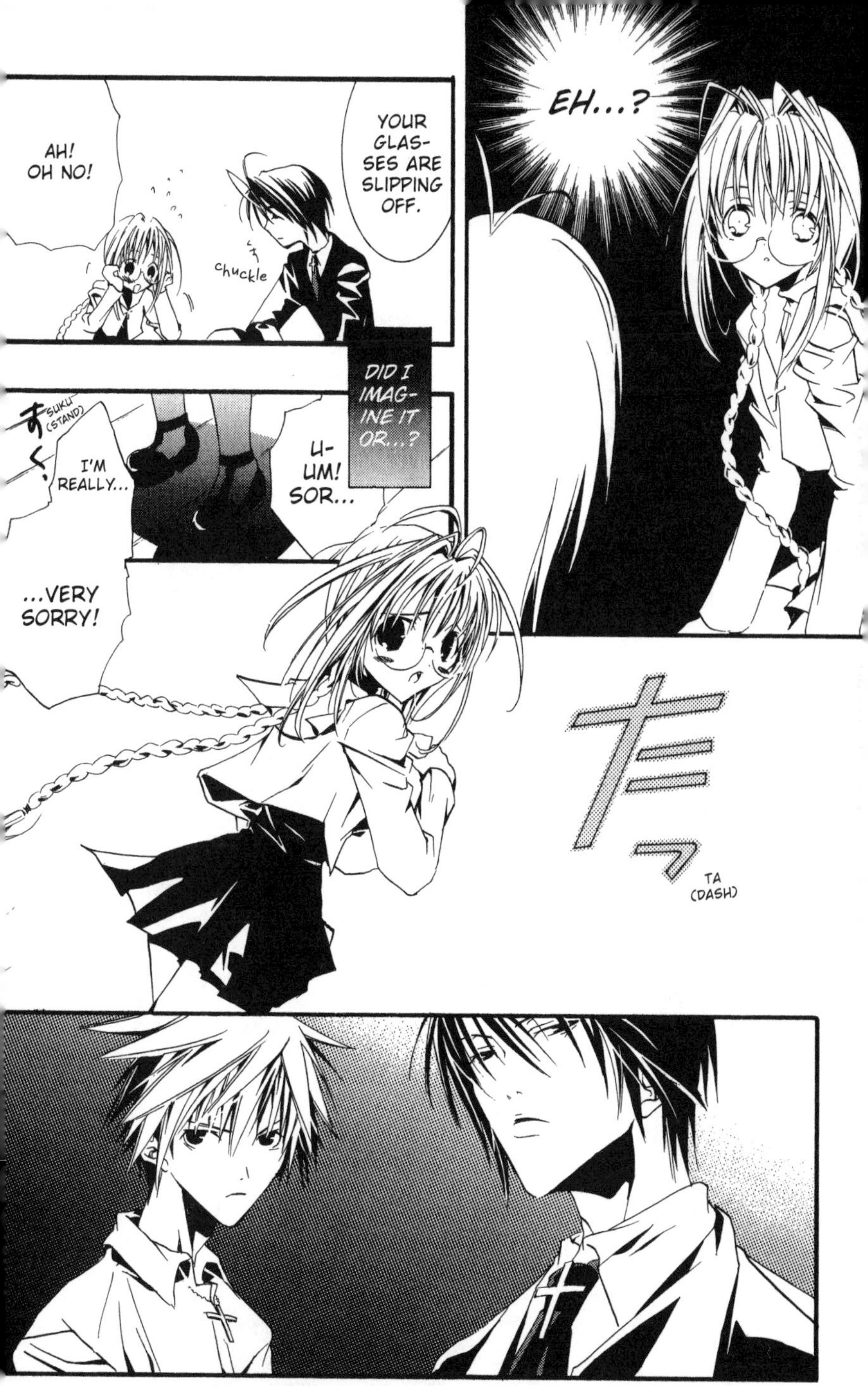
EH...?
YOUR GLASSES ARE SLIPPING OFF.
chuckle
AH! OH NO!
DID I IMAGINE IT OR...?
U-UM! SOR...
I'M REALLY...
すく SUKU (STAND)
...VERY SORRY!
タラ
TA (DASH)

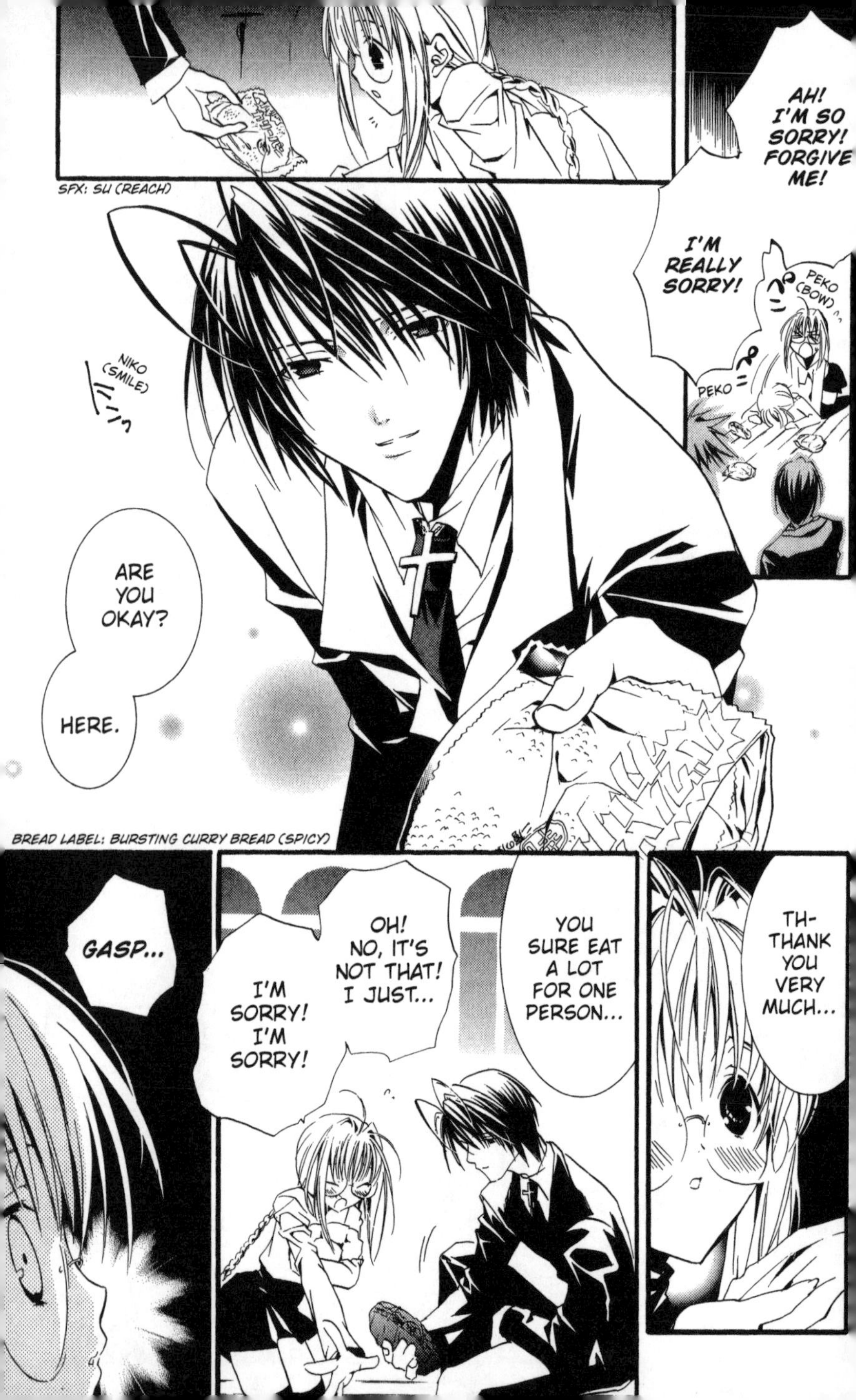
AH! I'M SO SORRY! FORGIVE ME!
SFX: SU (REACH)
I'M REALLY SORRY!
PEKO (BOW)
PEKO
NIKO (SMILE)
ARE YOU OKAY?
HERE.
BREAD LABEL: BURSTING CURRY BREAD (SPICY)
TH-THANK YOU VERY MUCH...
YOU SURE EAT A LOT FOR ONE PERSON...
OH! NO, IT'S NOT THAT! I JUST...
I'M SORRY! I'M SORRY!
GASP...

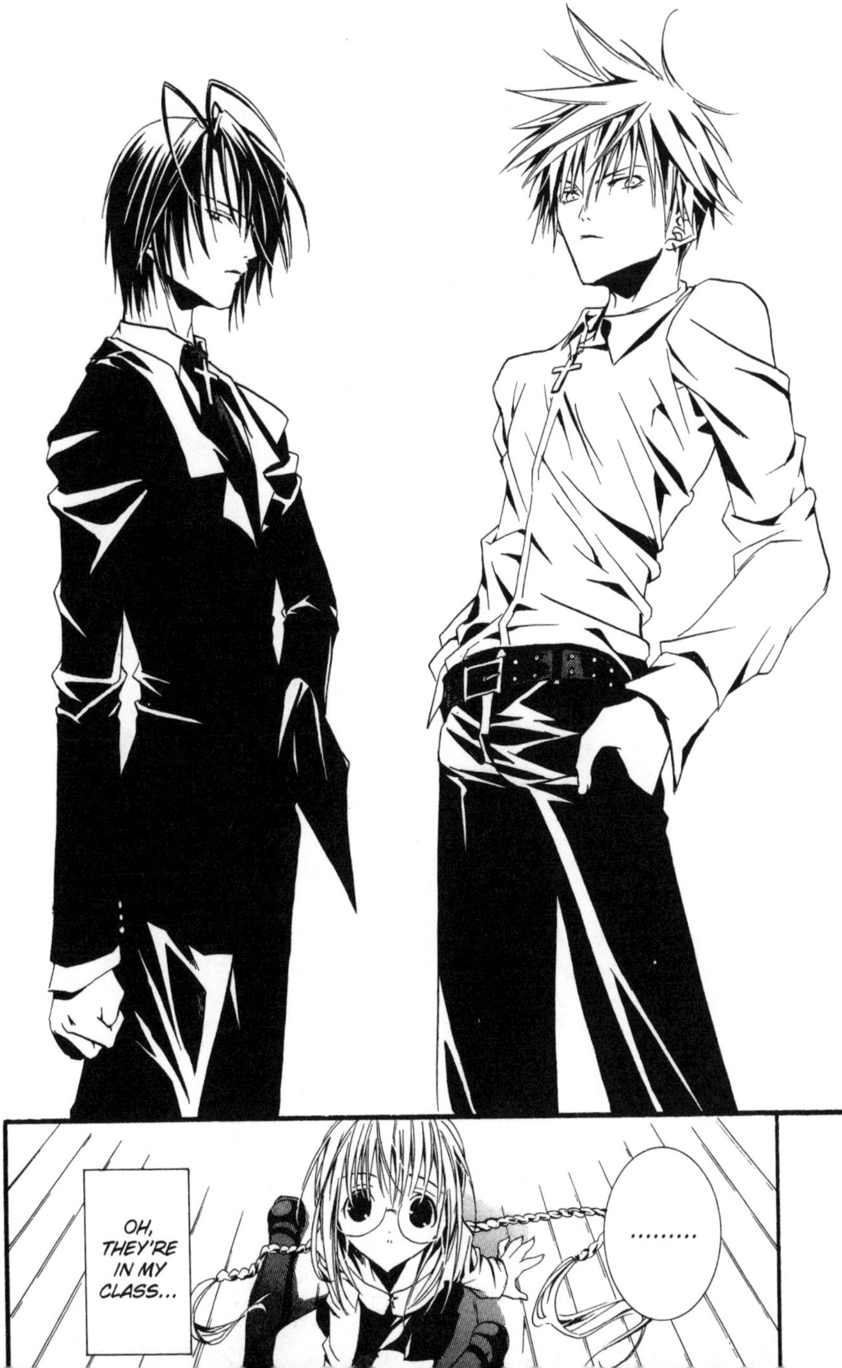
....
OH, THEY'RE IN MY CLASS...

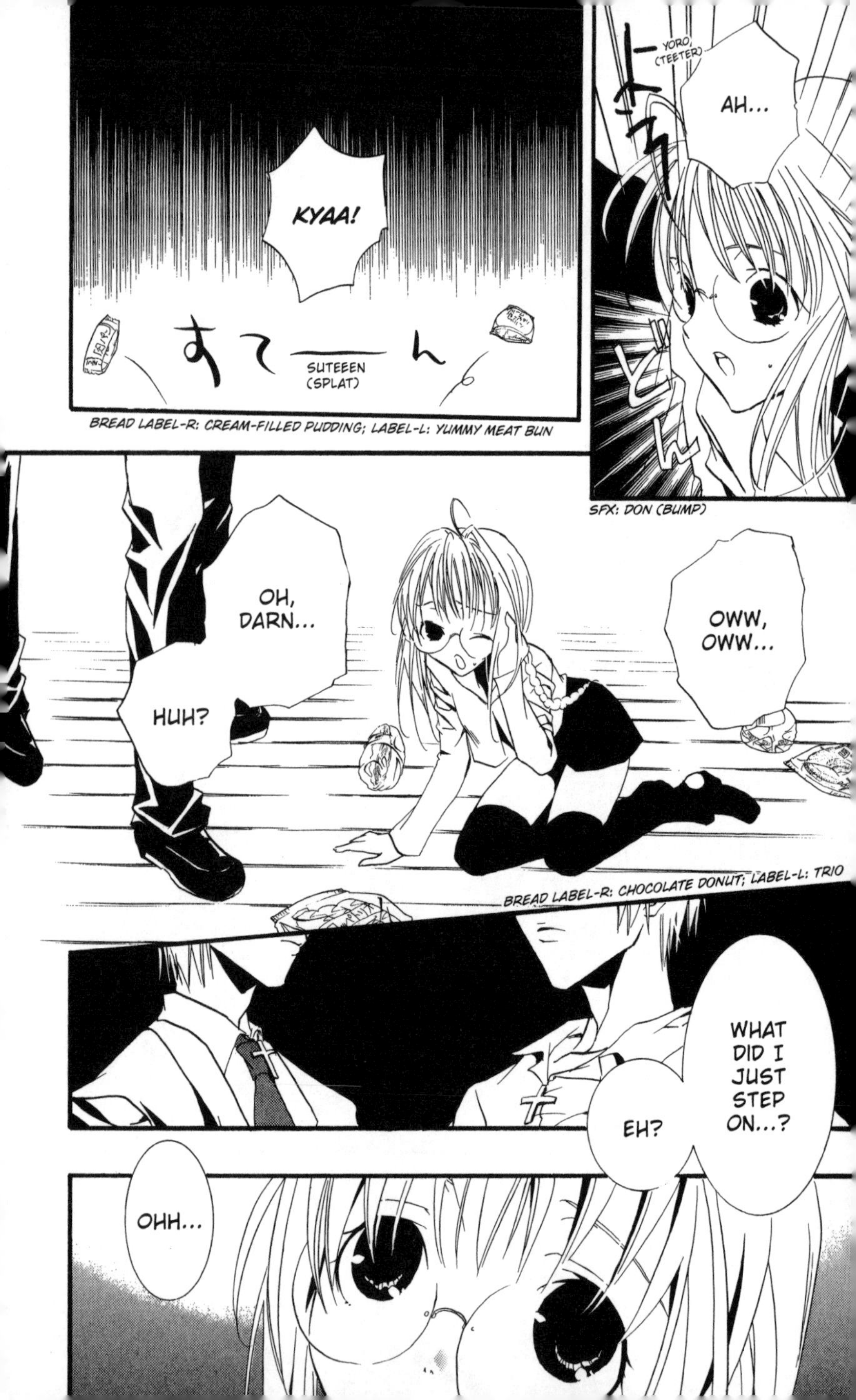
YORO (TEETER)
AH...
SFX: DON (BUMP)
KYAA!
すて——ん
SUTEEEN (SPLAT)
BREAD LABEL-R: CREAM-FILLED PUDDING; LABEL-L: YUMMY MEAT BUN
OWW, OWW...
OH, DARN...
HUH?
BREAD LABEL-R: CHOCOLATE DONUT; LABEL-L: TRIO
WHAT DID I JUST STEP ON...?
EH?
OHH...

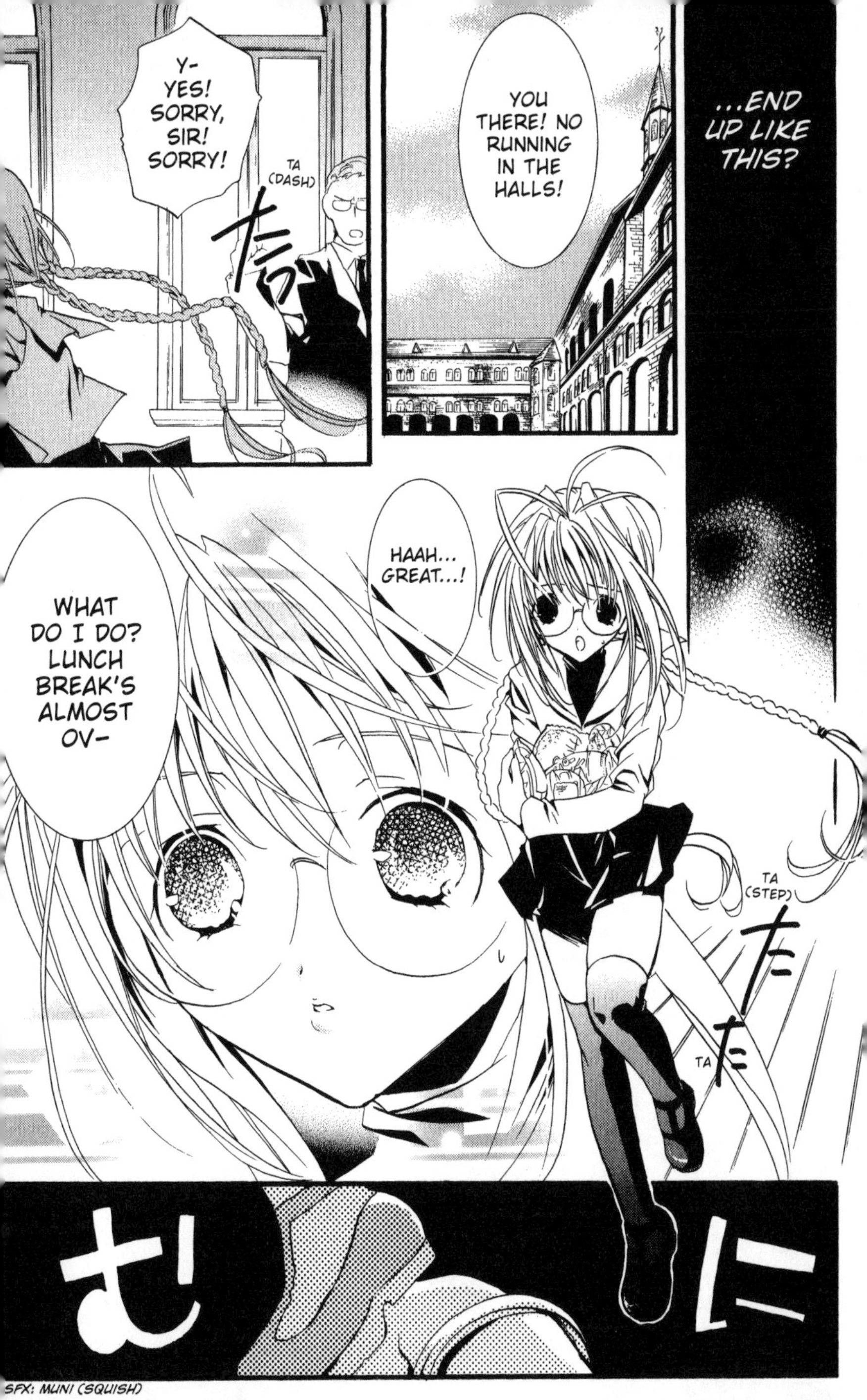
...END UP LIKE THIS?
YOU THERE! NO RUNNING IN THE HALLS!
Y- YES! SORRY, SIR! SORRY!
TA (DASH)
HAAH... GREAT...!
WHAT DO I DO? LUNCH BREAK'S ALMOST OV-
TA (STEP)
TA
SFX: MUNI (SQUISH)

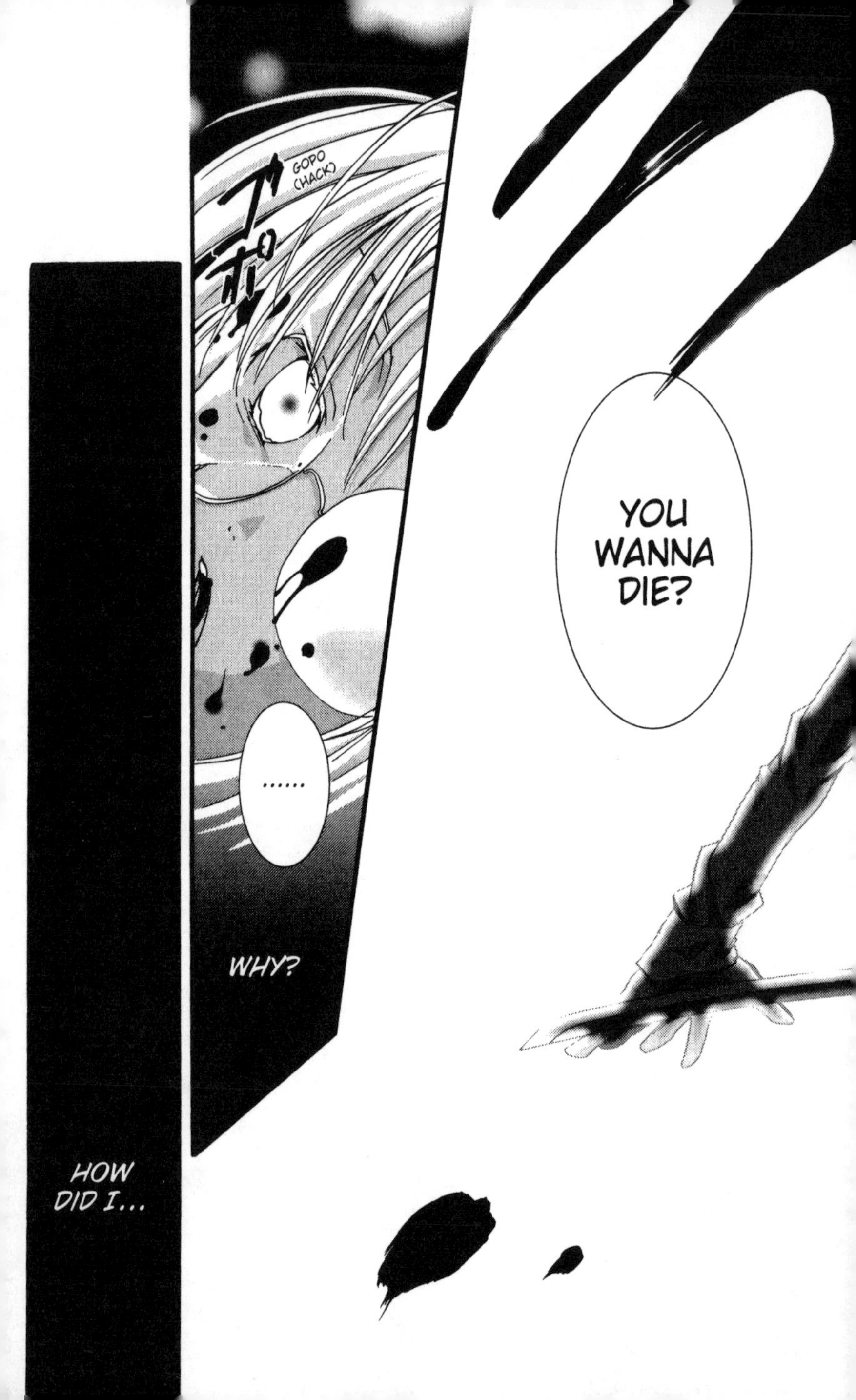
YOU WANNA DIE?
GOPO (HACK)
......
WHY?
HOW DID I...

PAYMENT : 1

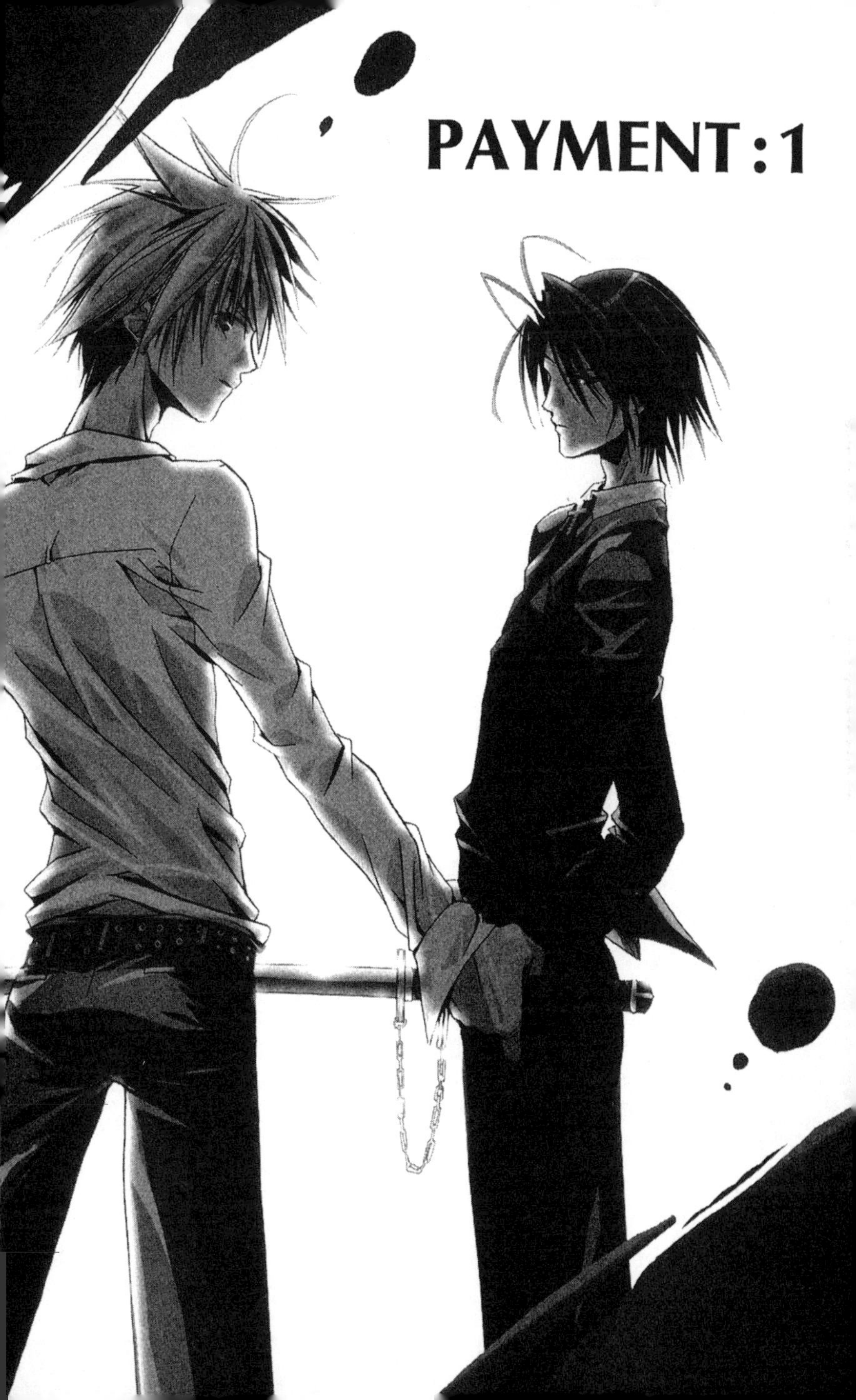

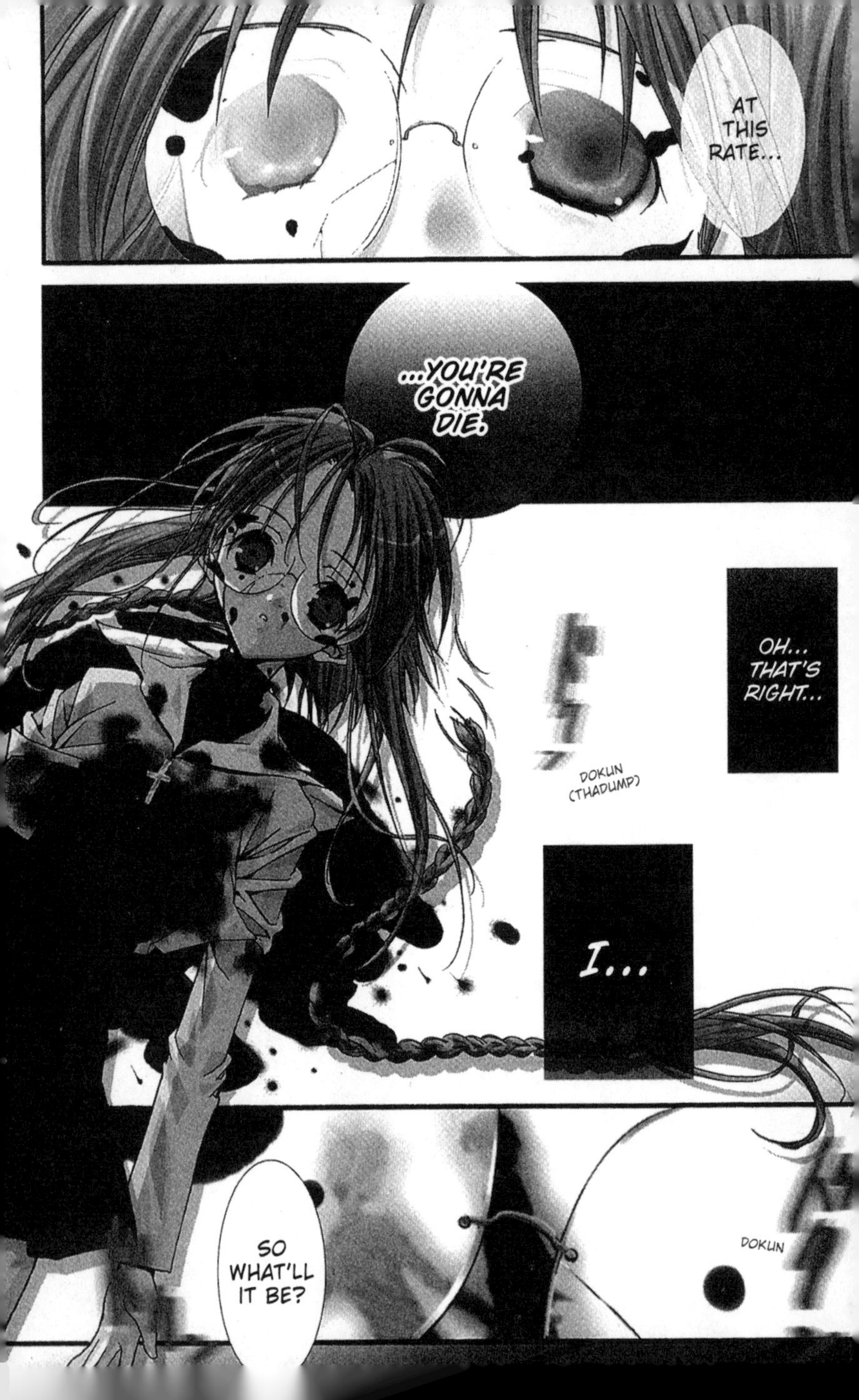
AT THIS RATE...
...YOU'RE GONNA DIE.
OH... THAT'S RIGHT...
DOKUN (THADUMP)
I...
DOKUN
SO WHAT'LL IT BE?

ZOMBIE-LOAN

Three teens spin a soulful tale of death and resurrection.

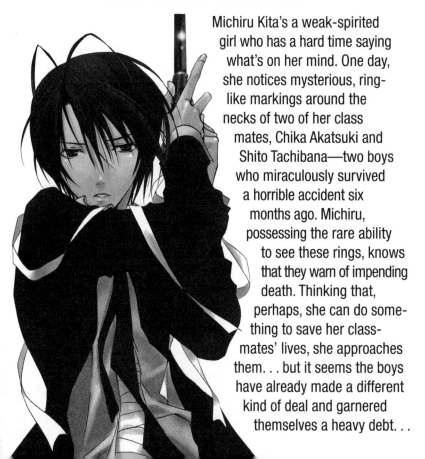

Michiru Kita's a weak-spirited girl who has a hard time saying what's on her mind. One day, she notices mysterious, ring-like markings around the necks of two of her classmates, Chika Akatsuki and Shito Tachibana—two boys who miraculously survived a horrible accident six months ago. Michiru, possessing the rare ability to see these rings, knows that they warn of impending death. Thinking that, perhaps, she can do some-thing to save her class-mates' lives, she approaches them. . . but it seems the boys have already made a different kind of deal and garnered themselves a heavy debt. . .

Dealing with the dead is even worse than dealing with the devil!

OLDER TEEN

OT

L V

- ISBN-13: 978-0-7595-2353-1
- ISBN-10: 0-7595-2353-3
- $10.99 USD/$12.75 CAN/£5.99 UK
- October 2007

Welcome from Yen Press!

This little teaser you hold in your hands is meant to whet your appetite for some of the fantastic licenses we have on tap for later this year. From sleuths to shinigami, dark fantasy, and even a bit of fanservice—you can look forward to a taste of everything, and what we hope you'll come to expect from us is the highest quality treatment of the material all around.

Our goal at Yen Press is to give you a reading experience as close to the original as possible, short of outright teaching you Japanese. We'll fret over every little sound effect, not only giving you the English equivalent but also a literal translation so you can "hear" the cadence being evoked. We'll battle amongst ourselves to strike just the right balance between literal translation and adaptation of the dialogue to give you the truest rendering. Did somebody break down and cry in the preparation of this material for you. . .?

Probably.

But it was worth it. . . because we just love manga that much.

Enjoy!

YEN PRESS MANGA TEASER

FALL 2007 SAMPLER COPYRIGHTS/CREDITS PAGE

WWW.YENPRESS.COM

ZOMBIE-LOAN
Story & Art: **PEACH-PIT**
Translation: **Christine Schilling**

Black God
Story: **Dall-Young Lim**
Art: **Sung-Woo Park**
Translation: **Christine Schilling**
Logo Design: **Kirk Benshoff**

Spiral: The Bonds of Reasoning
Story: **Kyo Shirodaira**
Art: **Eita Mizuno**
Translation: **Christine Schilling**
Logo Design: **Kirk Benshoff**

ALICE on Deadlines
Story & Art: **Shirō Ihara**
Translation: **Christine Schilling**
Logo Design: **EunKyung Kim**

TEEN
T
LV

OLDER TEEN
OT
LNSV

Yen Press™